An Official Whitman® Guidebook

The Official Whitman Statehood Quarters Collector's Handbook

Kenneth Bressett

Past President, American Numismatic Association

Whitman Coin Guides

St. Martin's Press ≋ New York

Title page coin courtesy of Whitman Coin Guides

www.stmartins.com

ISBN 0-312-97804-9
ISBN 1-58238-095-3

First Edition: July 2000

10 9 8 7 6 5 4 3 2 1

This book is dedicated to the men and women of the Citizens Commemorative Coin Advisory Committee, who were largely responsible for the recommendation and adoption of the 50 State Quarters program.

Contents

1

The United States Mint
50 State Quarters™ Program

Americans are proud of their country, of their heritage, and especially of the state in which they live. Such pride is rooted in the very origin of this nation, forged by the thirteen independent colonies that joined together to form what became the United States of America. Everyone longs to be part of a unique and distinct association, and loyalty to one's state is part of that kind of dedication.

Although united as a nation, each state is still independent enough to always be recognized as a separate entity. State pride is expressed in many ways. Each has its own state flag, a recognizable license plate for motor vehicles, a significant bird, flower, and perhaps a song. Now something new and exciting is happening throughout the land: a program whereby each state is honored with a national coin telling about the part that each has played in the history of this great country.

Take a careful look at your pocket change and you will be likely to find one or two of the new Statehood quarters. They were first minted and placed in circulation in 1999, and more of them are being made as fast as the United States Mint can produce them. Every ten weeks a new design is put into use, and a different state is honored. The effect of this program is cumulative. By the end of 2008 all fifty states will have been recognized on a special commemorative quarter, and all 50 different coins should be circulating freely throughout the land.

The United States Mint 50 State Quarters program was begun on December 1, 1997, when President William Jefferson Clinton signed a bill titled The 50 State Quarters Program Act, providing for the re-design of the reverse of the quarter dollar with 50 different designs emblematic of each of the 50 states. The coins are all to be issued in the sequence in which the states became part of the United States of America.

Statehood quarters will be made to honor all 50 states and will be produced in the order in which each state joined the union.

To make more room on the reverse of the commemorative quarters for each state's design, Congress also separately authorized the Mint to move certain design elements from the reverse (back or "tails" side) of the coin to the obverse (front or "heads" side), and vice versa, thus creating a new quarter obverse design. Changes to the obverse were kept minimal to avoid confusion, and to retain the familiar image of President George Washington. The state designs are displayed only on the reverse side of the quarters. In order to accommodate the new state designs, the words UNITED STATES OF AMERICA, QUARTER DOLLAR, LIBERTY, and IN GOD WE TRUST have been moved from the reverse to the obverse.

The program to honor the individual states was officially launched on January 8, 1998, when Treasury Secretary Robert E. Rubin issued letters to the governors of the five states that were to be recognized with commemorative coins in 1999. Those states, the first to sign the Declaration of Independence, were Delaware, Pennsylvania, New Jersey, Georgia, and Connecticut. The letter outlined the parameters and process for selecting state coin designs and requested an early response so that coinage could begin as quickly as possible. Target date for release of the first coin, that of Delaware, was set for January 1999. The enthusiasm shown by each of the states immediately insured that the Mint's tight schedule could be met both then and for all subsequent coins in the series.

Encouragement for the 50 state commemorative program was voiced by members of the coin collecting community as early as 1996 when numismatists (coin collectors) testified before Congress about the benefits that could be achieved by changing the designs on American coins to reflect the heritage of the country. The movement quickly gained congressional support and was endorsed by members of the Treasury Department. The quarter dollar was chosen as the coin for this program because it circulates widely and is available to all Americans. In addition, the large size of the quarter provides adequate space for the state design.

The authorizing Act states: "Congress finds that it is appropriate and timely to honor the unique Federal Republic of 50 States that comprise the United States; and to promote the diffusion of knowledge among the youth of the United States about the individual states, their history and geography, and the rich diversity of the national heritage; and to encourage young people and their families to collect memorable tokens of all the states for the face value of the coins."

Proof sets are packaged in a variety of ways. They are only sold in sets, and are only available from the United States Mint during the year of issue.

Each coin is marked with a letter designating where production took place: P for the Philadelphia Mint, D for the Denver Mint, or S for the San Francisco Mint. Production of coins made for circulation is carried on at the United States Mint in Philadelphia, Pennsylvania, and at the branch mint in Denver, Colorado. Specially made Proof versions of each issue are also produced at the branch mint in San Francisco, California. Proof pieces, which are essentially made only for collectors, differ from circulation coins in that their designs are impressed much more sharply and their surfaces have a perfect mirror-like finish. Proof (or Specimen) coins are not issued for circulation and are sold by the Mint only during the year in which they are made.

SCOPE OF THE AGENDA

The 50 State Quarter program will continue over a ten-year period, with five different designs being issued each year. Public Law 105-124 also provides that "If any additional state is admitted into the Union before the end of the ten-year period, the Secretary of the Treasury may issue quarter dollar coins, in accordance with this subsection, with a design which is emblematic of such state during any one year of such ten-year period, in addition to the quarter dollar coins issued during such year."

The District of Columbia and our nation's capital were not overlooked in the original legislature. The authorizing law only called for quarters to honor the 50 states. On April 1, 1998, Representative Eleanor Holmes-Norton (D-DC) introduced a bill to extend the program by one year to include other entities, such as American Samoa, the District of Columbia, Guam, Yap (in the Federated States of Micronesia), Puerto Rico, and the U.S. Virgin Islands.

In light of the widespread popularity of the Statehood quarter program, and the degree of enthusiasm that citizens have shown for these special coins, it seems inevitable that additional coins will be made to recognize one or more of the qualifying entities. The District of Columbia is almost certain to be the first so honored. It is also possible that other places as remote as the island of Yap or Guam could be included.

COST OF THE QUARTERS PROGRAM

There is no actual net cost to the U.S. taxpayer for the quarters. The cost to manufacture a circulating quarter is about five cents, providing the government with a profit of 20 cents per quarter. According to a Treasury feasibility study, demand for circulating quarters by collectors, beyond normal demand, will range from 1.5 to 3 billion quarters each year over the life of the program. This demand will generate an estimated profit of $2.6 to $5.1 billion over ten years. All costs of manufacturing and engraving associated with the program will be offset by this profit.

Once the coins are manufactured by the U.S. Mint they are shipped through the Federal Reserve System to various banks throughout the country. When the quarters reach your local bank they might be stored in bags of 4,000 coins with a face value of $1,000, or they might be wrapped in rolls for more convenient use. Some banks willingly sell bags or rolls of coins to customers, while others resist or have a policy of not providing such a service. Anyone who is interested in purchasing quantities of the new Statehood quarters should inquire at their local bank to see if arrangements can be made to secure such coins.

Throughout the ten-year period of production only new-style quarters will be manufactured. These quarters have the same status as the old "eagle" coins, and are legal tender for all commercial transactions. They are the same size and weight as the older quarters, and will be accepted in all vending machines. The standard diameter of each coin is 24.26mm, thickness is 1.75mm, and the edge is reeded.

Unlike the very old Washington quarters that were produced prior to 1965, none of the pieces now made for circulation are made of silver. They have a center core of copper with an outer coating of copper-nickel clad, the composition of which is 8.33 percent nickel and the balance pure copper. The only exceptions to this are the special collector's coins made at the San Francisco Mint for Proof sets, where one version is made of silver. The silver Proof coins can only be purchased from the Mint during the year of issue, and they are only sold in special sets at a premium price.

At present there are no plans to continue making more of the old-style Washington quarters until after the ten-year commemoration program is completed. As the ten years pass, there will be a gradual change in the variety of coins that will be seen in circulation. The old quarters will eventually be in the minority and the new Statehood quarters will be seen more frequently. At the end of the 50 State Quarters program the Mint could return to the traditional Washington quarter design with an eagle on the reverse, or an entirely new design could be adopted.

COLLECTING OPPORTUNITIES

The 50 state commemorative quarters are intended to circulate freely throughout the entire country. They are not made for use only in the state they commemorate, but can be found all over the country so that everyone has an opportunity to see and use them. The coins are distributed by banks through normal channels and will eventually become available to everyone who simply searches through their pocket change. It will not always be possible to find perfect pieces in your change because coins are subject to wear or abrasions once they enter circulation. In selecting coins for a collection it is always wise to save the most perfect pieces available.

Those who enjoy saving coins in choice Uncirculated (new) condition may purchase select specimens through coin dealers who charge a premium for the service they provide. During the year of manufacture coins may also be purchased directly from the Mint in sets. Both Uncirculated and Proof specimens are available through these channels but always at prices somewhat higher than face value.

Coins appeal to collectors of all ages.

Many collectors, young and old alike, find it rewarding and challenging to save one coin of each design and mintmark taken directly from circulation. These can be stored in a variety of ways, the most convenient being a collecting board, map, or album with spaces for one of each date, mintmark, and design. Such holders are available for purchase through many sources including coin dealers, bookstores, and the Mint itself. Complete sets of the 50 Statehood quarters will not be available from any source until 2008.

No one can predict the future availability or value of any of the state coins. It is the intention of the Mint to make these coins as prevalent as possible so that every American can enjoy seeing them in circulation. It is hoped that they will become a means of spreading knowledge about the history of the country in a way that will touch the lives of all of its citizens.

Some of the first issues of the Statehood quarters that were minted in 1999 were limited to quantities in the range of 300 to 350 million pieces before the Mint realized just how heavy the demand would be for the coins in circulation. Production was increased accordingly for later issues, but it was too late to correct the early shortages. As a result of this, coins of Delaware, Pennsylvania, and New Jersey may eventually be difficult to find because no more of the early issues of any of these coins will ever again be made.

Public interest in the Statehood quarters began as soon as the coins reached circulation and has never abated. It was not only the old-line collectors who wanted to save these coins, but a whole new generation of people who had never before taken any interest in coinage designs. Many people began to see coins in a whole new light, and to appreciate them as something more than just a means to purchase small items or make change. The role of coins as an art form and educational tool was at last being noticed by more than the established numismatic community.

People of all ages have taken up the challenge of assembling sets of the new quarters. Schoolchildren trade them like baseball cards, and adults are learning that they can exchange their Denver Mint quarters for Philadelphia Mint pieces by sending them to friends in other parts of the country. Even though these coins circulate freely throughout the nation, it is uncommon to find the Philadelphia coins west of the Mississippi, or Denver coins in the East.

The 50 State Quarters program has been a rousing success for the U.S. Mint and the hobby of numismatics. Millions of people are collecting the Statehood quarters in some fashion or another, be it in plain or fancy albums, a wide array of colorfully varied coin maps, or the family cookie jar. A significant portion of those millions of people is beginning to collect other United States coins as well. Those who take time to explore and learn more about the fascinating hobby of coin collecting will find that a rich array of knowledge and entertainment awaits them.

PUBLIC INVOLVMENT IN THE PROGRAM

The new quarters have touched the lives of all Americans. Many view them with pride, knowing that their state has been honored. Others are eagerly awaiting the time when their state will be recognized, and some are actively involved in the design process to help create or select an appropriate commemoration for their state.

Youngsters are particularly fond of the Statehood quarters and add new pieces to their sets as quickly as each design is released. The availability and modest cost of these coins make them ideal for a beginning collector. At the end of the Mint's program a full set of all 50 issues will have a face value of $12.50 and will still be as spendable as the coins were when first saved. In addition to being an interesting and novel way to save money, these coins are also educational, instructing young and old alike in things about their country that they might otherwise overlook.

Perhaps it is the easy availability of the new quarters that makes them so appealing to everyone. Perhaps it is the novelty of something never before encountered by the general public, or the hope that one or more of these may become so much in demand that values will rise and the coins will be a good investment. Surely there are many reasons why people save these coins, but the most compelling is the challenge of eventually finding a complete set of all 50 states, and of learning more about our great country through them.

The United States Mint is working closely with educational organizations across the country to develop educational materials and an interactive website, enabling educators to bring the rich history of the Mint and facts about how the 50 State Quarters program honors the American union to their classrooms. Up-to-date information about each new issue and other facts about the program can be found on the Mint's special website at usmint.gov.

WILL ALL COIN DESIGNS BE CHANGED?

The overwhelming popularity and success of the Mint's 50 State Quarters program has inspired many people to think about the possibility of changing the designs on all United States coins. Many Americans have never seen or even heard about coins other than those that have been in use in this country for as long as most people can remember. Many people had never given thought to what could be done to change designs on our nation's money until they encountered the Statehood quarters. Now they are wondering if, or why, our other coins could not be similarly improved.

Most current United States coins feature the image of a president. This is a recent custom that was started only within the last century. Prior to 1909, all American coins had some representation of Liberty as the principal design. In some cases she was portrayed as an Indian, but no actual portrait of anyone living or dead was ever considered for the design. Then in 1909 the Mint broke with tradition and placed a portrait of Abraham Lincoln on the one-cent coin in honor of the centenary of his birth. That design was continued for the next 50 years until the reverse was changed in 1959 to mark the 150th anniversary. At that time an image of the Lincoln Memorial was added to the coin as a double tribute to the beloved president.

Many people feel that it would be appropriate to again redesign the Lincoln cent for the bicentennial of Lincoln's birth in 2009. They point to the fact that this would come at the end of the quarter program and at an ideal time to continue the momentum of coinage design changes. Some other presidential coin designs are nearly as old as the cent: The nickel with Thomas Jefferson's portrait was introduced in 1939; the Roosevelt dime came along in 1946; and Kennedy half dollars were first made in 1964.

Countries around the world normally change the designs on their coins and paper money regularly, sometimes as often as every year or two. Switzerland is one notable exception to this and is perhaps the only country that has used the same designs longer than those on United States coins. There are no legal reasons why the designs on American coins cannot be changed at this time. The biggest objection seems to be a resistance to removing the images of famous Americans, and the question of who could replace them. Proponents of change feel that there are politically neutral themes that could be used to good advantage. Such a plan was recently put into place when the Susan B. Anthony dollar was replaced with a coin honoring a Native American woman.

The Susan B. Anthony dollar failed in its appeal to the public as an acceptable design or functional coin.

The design of this outstanding new coin was selected in national competition from among 120 submissions that were considered by a panel appointed by Treasury Secretary Robert Rubin. The chosen motif depicts Sacagawea, a young Native American Shoshone, as conceived by artist Glenna Goodacre and modeled on a living Shoshone woman, Randy 'L He-dow Teton. On her back she carries Jean Baptiste, her infant son. The reverse shows an eagle in flight designed by Mint Engraver Thomas D. Rogers, Sr.

An example of a carefully selected design and composition.

The symbolism of the new dollar exemplifies the spirit of Liberty, Peace, and Freedom shown by Sacagawea in her conduct as interpreter and guide to explorers Meriwether Lewis and William Clark during their famed journey westward from the Great Northern Plains to the Pacific. These coins have a distinctive golden color and a plain edge to distinguish them from other denominations or coins of a similar size. The new coins are made from an alloy of 88.5 percent copper, plus zinc, manganese, and nickel. The change in composition and appearance was mandated under the United States Dollar Coin Act of 1997.

When the Sacagawea dollars were first made in 2000, they represented a major breakthrough in thinking about what kinds of designs can be successfully used on American coins. The trend of the future might well be away from past presidents and toward a new era of artistic designs reflecting more of the proud history of the country.

2

History of the United States Quarter Dollar

The story of American money, which covers a period of more than three centuries, began when early settlers in New England carried on their fur trade with the Indians through the use of wampum beads fashioned from quahog clam shells. Beaver skins, wampum, and, in Virginia, tobacco, soon became the commonly accepted media of exchange for all other available commodities. Early American immigrants, in fact, had little use for any coined money at first; however, when traders arrived from foreign lands, coins were usually demanded in payment for goods.

Any foreign coins were usually accepted, such as French *louis*, English *guineas*, German *thalers*, Dutch *ducats*, and various Spanish coins, including *doubloons* and the particularly notable "milled dollar" or piece-of-eight. The Spanish dollar became such an important monetary unit throughout the colonial period that even after the Revolutionary War the dollar and its fractional parts continued to circulate with official sanction until 1857.

Spanish two reales *coins served the country for many years before quarter-dollar coins were authorized.*

Before the establishment of the United States Mint in 1792, the country had no standard federal coinage of its own. In the period from 1776 to 1788 several individual states took it upon themselves to manufacture their own coins, but these coins saw only limited circulation, and were used mostly in the New England area. Money from any available source, especially European silver coins, made up the bulk of specie used in daily commerce.

The Articles of Confederation, adopted March 1, 1781, provided that Congress should have the sole right to regulate the alloy and value of coin struck by its own authority or by that of the respective states. Each state therefore had the right to coin money, but Congress served as a regulating authority. New Hampshire was the first state to consider coinage, but few if any coins were placed in circulation. The only known specimens made by that state bear the date 1776.

On April 2, 1792, a bill was passed providing "that the money of account of the United States should be expressed in dollars or units, dismes or tenths, cents or hundredths, and milles or thousands; a disme being the tenth part of a dollar, a cent the hundredth part of a dollar, a mille the thousandth part of a dollar." Denominations specified in the act were the gold Eagle, half Eagle and quarter Eagle; the silver dollar, half dollar, quarter dollar, disme and half disme; and a copper cent and half cent.

It is interesting to note that although a decimal plan was proposed for the monetary system, not all of the adopted denominations are strictly decimal in nature. A purer form would have used twenty-cent, forty-cent, two-dollar, and four-dollar coins. The decision to divide the dollar into half- and quarter-dollar units was based on the longstanding practice of using Spanish colonial coins that were divided into eighths.

To meet the growing demand for minor coins, a mint building was erected in Philadelphia and equipment quickly installed. Production in 1793 consisted of copper cents and half cents. Coinage of dollars, half dollars, dimes, and half dimes was begun in 1794, but it was not until 1796 that production of quarter-dollar coins was undertaken. At that time there was no consideration of a twenty-cent coin, and indeed none were made until a failed attempt in 1875–76 produced a few of the unpopular coins.

Unlike the twenty-cent pieces, the quarter-dollar coins have been successful and popular with the public ever since the first pieces were made in 1796. In fact, they are the most used coins in circulation today and require an annual coinage of one to two billion pieces. By way of contrast, fewer than 50 million half-dollar coins are made each year.

"TWO BITS" AND OTHER COINS

Throughout the Colonial years, Americans became accustomed to using the Spanish dollar and its fractional parts, the *real*, the *medio* (half *real*), and especially the two-*reales* and four-*reales* coins. Prior to establishment of the Mint, the predecessors of our modern quarters were the English *shillings*, Spanish-American two *reales*, or other European coins that were approximately equivalent in size and value to a quarter of the Spanish dollar.

The piece-of-eight, as its name implies, was divided into eighths and denominated as one, two, and four *reales*. The minting of those coins in this hemisphere took place in the silver-rich countries of Bolivia, Chile, Colombia, Mexico, Guatemala, and Peru. Coins from Mexico were particularly apt to flow north and end up in America, where they continued to circulate as legal tender until 1857.

When small change was not available to the colonists, the large and more plentiful eight *reales* coins were sometimes cut in half or into smaller pie-shaped fractional parts to facilitate commercial transactions. One *real* (an eighth of a Spanish dollar) was known as a "bit" and was equal in value to 12½ cents. Two *reales*, or "two bits," were equal in value to 25 cents. When the first American quarters were made, they quickly acquired the same nickname, and the term "two bits" was in popular use in this country for over two centuries and is occasionally heard even today.

When small change was not available, the large and plentiful eight reales *coins were cut into pie-shaped fractional parts to facilitate trade. Two* reales, *or "two-bits," were equal in value to a quarter dollar or 25 cents.*

THE HISTORY OF U.S. QUARTER DESIGNS

Though the United States Mint began making coins for the young country in 1793, for some unknown reason quarter-dollar coins were not attempted until 1796. However, as early as 1792 an experimental pattern quarter was made as a proposal for that denomination. Joseph Wright designed the model intended for the original quarter dollar.

Many consider the 1792 pattern quarter to be one of the most artistic designs ever proposed for an early American coin.

Wright was George Washington's choice for the position of the first Chief Engraver of the United States Mint, and he probably would have been appointed if he had not died shortly after this beautiful design was created in 1792. Only four specimens of this interesting pattern still exist. Two of them are made of copper, and two were struck in white metal. For some reason this design was never adopted, even though many believe that it was one of the most artistic ever proposed for any early American coin.

The first federally authorized quarters were struck by the United States Mint in 1796. Silver used to make them came mainly from worn foreign coins that were deposited at the Mint to be made into U.S. coinage. Very little came from commercial mines in this country. The design used on the first quarters was the same as that used on other silver denominations of that year. The obverse features a bust of Liberty; the reverse shows an eagle perched on clouds and surrounded by a wreath. Robert Scot prepared the dies.

The first United States quarters did not include any indication of value. They were accepted by weight as being equal to the Spanish coins they replaced.

It is interesting to note that the first quarter coins did not have any indication of value on them. They were slightly larger in diameter than the quarters we use today but a bit thinner, and they contained more silver. Only 6,146 quarters were made that first year, and today they are considered to be among the rarest and most valuable early American coins.

From that slow beginning, it would be another eight years before more quarters were made during the period from 1804 to 1807. When production started in earnest in 1815, it continued almost without interruption to the present.

A curious feature seen on the quarters of 1796 is in the arrangement of stars around the head of Liberty on the obverse of this coin. We are accustomed to seeing 13 stars on United States coins to honor the 13 original colonies, but this coin has 15 stars. The additional stars were in recognition of Vermont and Kentucky, which had joined the Union by the time these coins were made. The plan was to add a star for each new state that joined the Union, but it was soon realized that it would not be possible to recognize the entire country. In a sense, the 1796 quarter was the first commemorative quarter to honor any of the states and predates the current Statehood coins by over 200 years.

United States quarters have gone through several design changes since their introduction in 1796. In the early years, they followed the designs of other denominations using the head of Liberty, a seated figure of Liberty, and the Barber design that also appeared on the dime and half dollar from 1892 to 1916. In recent years the quarter has had its own special design not shared with any other denomination.

When the design of the quarter was changed in 1804, the denomination 25 c. was added to the reverse.

In 1804, the design of the quarter was changed and the eagle on the reverse replaced with a heraldic-style bird. This was done to conform to other United States coins of the period. The redesigned coins also included an indication of the denomination for the first time. Like its predecessor, the redesigned quarter weighed 6.74 grams and was composed of 0.8924 fine silver. At 27.5mm, the diameter was almost exactly the same as the still current Spanish-American two *reales* piece. Coins of this style were made from 1804 to 1807.

The next change in the appearance of the quarter came in 1815, when the head of Liberty was completely remodeled and a somewhat more lifelike eagle added to the reverse. John Reich was the designer of this attractive coin, which was made in most years from 1815 to 1828. The eagle on the reverse grasps a bundle of arrows indicating preparedness for war, and is perched on an olive branch indicating a desire for peace. The denomination 25 C. is beneath the eagle, and for the first time on any quarter-dollar coin the national motto E PLURIBUS UNUM has been added in the space above the eagle's head.

A variation in the quarter design was introduced in 1831 when dies were prepared by William Kneass. On these coins the motto was removed from above the eagle's head.

The design of the quarter underwent a minor revision in 1831 when Mint Engraver William Kneass modified the portrait of Liberty and sharpened details of the eagle and lettering. These changes were made at the same time that the diameter of the coin was reduced to better accommodate some of the new minting equipment that was being installed in the Mint. The more modern machinery was responsible for these coins being perfectly round and much better made than earlier pieces. The revised Liberty Cap design was in use from 1831 to 1838.

A major change in the life of the quarter occurred in 1838 when the weight was reduced to 6.68 grams. The fineness was increased to 90 percent pure silver to compensate for the difference in weight. The diameter was kept at the current standard of 24.3mm. At this time coinage was also extended to the newly opened New Orleans branch mint. Prior to this time all quarter-dollar coins had been made at the original United States Mint in Philadelphia. The design of the quarter was also completely changed at this time and the traditional head of Liberty replaced with a seated figure of Liberty holding a staff with cap in one hand, the other hand resting on the national shield.

Liberty Seated quarters were made from 1838 to 1891 with only minor changes and modifications to the basic design.

In retrospect it may seem strange to many that Liberty is portrayed on these coins holding a cloth cap. The symbolism of such an item is lost today, but it was perfectly understood in the earlier days of this country and was used on many coins. It has its origins in ancient times when the hat, properly known as a Phrygian cap, was awarded to a slave who had earned his or her freedom. American and French artists of the period were fond of finding ways to include the Phrygian cap in their designs that represented Liberty or Freedom.

Changes to the Liberty Seated design were minor, but did occur frequently throughout the life span of this quarter. The first came in 1853 when the price of silver rose to a point where the quarter became worth more than 25 cents. To avoid the threat of these coins being melted for their extra value, the weight was lowered to 6.22 grams. The situation was similar to that faced by the nation in 1965, when silver coins were withdrawn from circulation because of the runaway price of silver.

Quarters were made to the lighter-weight standard starting in 1853. In an effort to clearly identify the new coins, the Mint placed small arrowheads on either side of the date and a burst of rays around the eagle on the reverse. The public seemed to accept the modified quarters without complaint, and in the following years, 1854 and 1855, the rays were removed from the reverse, leaving only the arrows at the date to identify the reduced-weight coins. By 1856 the incident was apparently forgotten or ignored, and the original coin design was restored and used for the next ten years.

During the time that these quarters were in use, thoughts about the Civil War were uppermost in everyone's mind. The conflict between northern and southern states was a tragedy that affected the entire nation. In 1863 sentiment about the war was reflected on America's coins through the inclusion of a new motto, IN GOD WE TRUST. The concept of using such a saying on coins originated with the Reverend M. R. Watkins of Ridleyville, Pennsylvania, who felt that adding a symbol of faith to our coinage would help bring comfort to a suffering nation. In a letter to Secretary Treasurer Salmon P. Chase, Reverend Watkins suggested that all United States coins should contain some form of recognition of God. In response to this the now-familiar motto was adopted and first used on the copper two-cent coins of 1864.

In 1866 it was felt that the religious motto should be added to other denominations, and the quarter design was again modified to accommodate the additional wording. Space was found above the eagle on the reverse of the coin where the motto was used thereafter. Yet another change came to the Liberty Seated quarters in 1873 and 1874 when arrows were again added at either side of the date. This time they were placed there to indicate another change in weight when it was increased from 6.22 grams to 6.25 grams.

By 1875 there was no longer any need to identify the new heavyweight coins, and the arrows were eliminated. From then until the end of coinage with the Liberty Seated design there were no further modifications. During the period of coinage from 1838 to 1891, billions of these quarters were made. They were struck at mints in Philadelphia, Carson City, New Orleans, and San Francisco. Today these are some of the most readily available early-date quarters, and examples are usually available at very reasonable prices for coins in grades up to Fine condition.

Quarters engraved by Charles Barber were the first to be identified with any artist's initials in the design.

In 1892 Mint Engraver Charles E. Barber was commissioned to design a completely new head of Liberty for use on the quarter, half dollar, and dime. He also revised the heraldic eagle into a pose that could be used on the quarter and half dollar, but was too large to fit on the dime. The stern features of the Barber head of Liberty seemed to instill confidence in the stability of these coins and were seen as a pleasant change from the Seated pieces that had gone out of fashion. Barber quarters were made each year from 1892 to 1916 and were struck at the mints in Philadelphia, San Francisco, Denver, and New Orleans. The designer's initial B can be found on the truncation of the neck of Liberty, and is the first time that any quarter was so identified by a designer.

World War I was the occasion for another change in design for the American quarter. In 1916 the quarter, dime, and half dollar were all re-designed to stay contemporary with modes of the times. The remarkable designs used on these quarters are the work of the talented American artist, Hermon MacNeil, who created the beautiful Liberty Standing figure seen on quarters made from 1916 to 1930. Two types of these quarters were made. The first, coined in 1916 and part of 1917, have no stars below the eagle on the reverse. Quarters of the second type were coined from 1917 to 1930, with the exception of 1922 when none were made. They were all struck at the Philadelphia, Denver, and San Francisco Mints. Those coined after 1924 have the date slightly recessed to prevent the wear that tended to obliterate the earlier dates.

Two styles of quarters were made showing Liberty standing. The first issued only in 1916 and 1917 was discontinued because of public criticism of Liberty's exposed breast.

When MacNeil's Liberty Standing quarters made their first appearance in 1916 they created quite a stir. The public was prepared for a change, but nothing as shocking as what they found on these coins. This time the figure of Liberty was naked above the waist. The symbolism was meant to show America as Mother to the world, but it failed public approval and was quickly changed in 1917 by the addition of a coat of mail, presumably as a protection from war.

Someone made a mistake when the die for this 1918-S quarter was being made. The date clearly shows 1917 underneath the current date.

The armor did not totally prevent one major wartime casualty to these quarters, which happened in 1918 when the mint was faced with a shortage of experienced workers. In the process of making dies for coins that year, someone mistakenly added a second date on top of the date that had already been pressed into the die. The result was a die that clearly showed the date 1918 on top of 1917, and the coins made from that die all showed the mistake. Only a few of those coins made it into circulation, and today they are avidly sought by collectors who gladly pay in excess of $1,000 each for specimens in any grade of condition.

The bust of President Washington used on this coin was copied from a life portrait sculpted by Jean Antoine Houdon.

Quarters displaying the head of George Washington are the type most familiar to Americans today. They were first issued for circulation in 1932 and have continued to be made in one form or another ever since. Throughout the years numerous changes and modifications have been made in this series, which is probably what makes them so popular with collectors. These quarters have been minted in Philadelphia, Denver, and San Francisco. Nearly all dates and mintmarks are still readily available in circulated grades of condition at modest prices and even Uncirculated coins dated after 1950 are not very expensive.

The George Washington quarters of 1932 were designed by John Flanagan, a New York sculptor who was allowed to include his initials JF at the base of Washington's neck. The original quarters were intended to be a circulating commemorative coin made in honor of the first president's birth. The design was an immediate success and the public demanded more such coins. After a hiatus of one year the presses started up again, making the coins in 1934 and every year thereafter. The popularity of this coin has never waned despite its longtime service in circulation and its numerous reincarnations.

Washington quarters were the first coins to be changed in 1965 when the government mandated that silver should be removed from circulating coinage. Prior to that, quarters had been composed of 90 percent silver, with a net content close to 0.1808 oz. of pure silver. The new composition introduced in 1965 was a clad "sandwich" of copper-nickel covering a core of pure copper. The substitute metal has proved to be a suitable choice that resists wear from circulation and has good color and weight.

COMMEMORATIVE QUARTERS

Commemorative Bicentennial quarters were made in 1975 and 1976. All of them have the dual dates 1776–1976, therefore no quarters are actually dated 1975.

In October of 1973 the Treasury announced open contests for the selection of suitable designs for the Bicentennial reverses of the quarter-, half-, and one-dollar coins, with $5,000 to be awarded to the winner of each. Twelve finalists were chosen, and from those the entry of Jack L.

Ahr was selected for the quarter reverse. It features a Colonial drummer facing left, with a victory torch encircled by thirteen stars at the upper left. Except for the dual dating, 1776–1976, the obverse remained unchanged. Only pieces with this dual dating were coined during 1975 and 1976. These coins were struck for general circulation in great numbers and can still be found in change with ease. Additional pieces were also made for inclusion in Mint sets of Uncirculated and Proof coins that were sold to the public at premium prices.

The current series of commemorative Statehood Washington quarters is a topic of interest to all Americans. The front of the coin has been changed to accommodate the revised wording that had to be moved from the reverse to make room for the 50 new designs that will honor each of the states. The modified obverse design is the work of Mint Engraver William Cousins, and in recognition of this his initials WC have been added to the truncation of Washington's neck adjacent to those of the original designer, John Flanagan.

The first collector's commemorative quarter was made in 1892 to celebrate the Columbian World's Fair and anniversary of the discovery of America. Since then circulating quarters have been made for the Bicentennial and Statehood series.

In addition to all of the quarters that have been made for use in daily circulation, there was also a commemorative coin made in 1893 to celebrate the famous World's Columbian Exposition in Chicago and to mark the four-hundredth anniversary of the discovery of America. An image of Queen Isabella of Spain was used on the obverse of that unusual coin, which is the only American coin to honor a foreign monarch.

OTHER KINDS OF QUARTERS

Quarter-dollar paper issues have played a lesser role in American history, but they too form an interesting part of our heritage. Early scrip notes often show a relationship to the Spanish "bit" or *real* system and are sometimes denominated as 6¼ or 12½ cents. During the Civil War and its aftermath, 25-cent notes helped offset the coin shortage. A colorful array of government-issued "fractional currency" notes that were used in place of quarters was made. These show a wide diversity in designs and were apparently well-received for many years as substitutes for the scarce coins.

At the time of the most critical shortage of quarters—during the Civil War—postage stamps were sometimes pressed into use as a substitute for coins. Some of them were passed from person to person in small envelopes; others were encased in mica-covered metal cases to protect the delicate paper. This necessary form of money lasted only a few years and was never a popular way to conduct business. The practice was abandoned as soon as there were again enough quarters in circulation to serve commercial needs.

COLLECTING QUARTERS

Acquiring quarters for your collection can be a difficult or not-so-difficult challenge. This is a long series of dates with many variables. Still, it is an engaging hobby and well worth the effort to find interesting specimens for a collection or set. Caution is advised for anyone starting to save these coins by date and mint. Some are very rare, some are very common, and prices can range from two or three dollars for recent issues to over $50,000 for a decent specimen of the first year of issue. It will not be possible to obtain uncirculated specimens of every date, as some of them are not available at any price. All of the early dates before 1831 are particularly difficult to find, even in worn condition.

The Liberty Seated quarters have never caught on as a collectible series. This is probably because there are so many different dates and mints to contend with. Most of today's collectors are content to have only a basic type set of the early quarters, and to concentrate on trying to obtain pieces that grade Very Fine or better. Investors seem to be attracted to choice Proof or Uncirculated pieces and are often willing to pay many times more than the prices for lower-grade coins to obtain the higher quality. The same can be said for Barber quarters, although the challenge of putting together a fairly complete set of dates is not quite as daunting as with the earlier coins.

Liberty Standing quarters were minted from 1916 through 1930. They are one of the most attractive of all modern coins and a favorite among collectors. Dealers and investors tend to avoid these pieces because they are among the most difficult of all coins to grade accurately. Caution is advised for anyone buying Uncirculated Liberty Standing quarters that have not been graded by an experienced dealer or collector.

Sets of circulated quarters, both Liberty Standing and Washington pieces, are fun to collect. There are some hard-to-find dates in the Standing series, but most of the more common pieces can be obtained at modest prices. All of the Washington coins are common and plentiful in all grades up to Brilliant Uncirculated. Hoards of old silver coins often contain at least one of each date and mint for the entire series, with the possible exception of 1932-D and 1932-S. Quarters made since 1965 are all readily available and make a great extension to any collection of Statehood quarters.

seems to be setting them aside rather than spending them as the government envisioned. As a result, some of the early designs can now be hard to find in circulation and are already beginning to have a premium value.

If the trend in hoarding continues, the Mint will probably have to work overtime to produce enough coins to meet normal commercial needs. An alternative would be to resume making more of the old-style Washington quarters in addition to the Statehood pieces, but at this time there are no such plans in the offing. Speculation is that the Statehood coin program will continue on schedule, and that everyone will have the chance to obtain as many of the quarters as they want with one important caveat: Get the coins you want as soon as they are released. Once the 10-week minting period is over for each state, no more of those coins will ever be made.

Whatever your goals, you will probably do well to save at least one of every available kind of Statehood coin that is issued. In doing this you will be assured that if any one of them becomes exceptionally valuable or hard to find, for whatever reason, you will have at least one of them in your holdings. In order to be sure that you have examples of each of the different issues you will have to know something about the coins and what to look for when they are issued.

Each of the 50 state designs will be used on quarters that are manufactured at the mints in Denver and Philadelphia. These different varieties can be easily identified by the mintmark that appears on the obverse of each coin. A letter D indicates that the coin was made at the branch mint in Denver. The letter P shows that it was made at the mint in Philadelphia. Different quantities of coins are apt to be produced at each of these mints, and because of this some may be scarcer than others. Mintmarks are important to collectors who value their coins in accordance to how scarce they are, and consider coins of different mints individually even though they may be of the same design.

All of the coins in the 50 State Quarters program will be manufactured at both the Denver and Philadelphia mints. The mintmark, D or P, on the obverse indicated which mint struck that particular coin.

3

The 50 State Quarters™ Program in Action

It's easy to collect the Statehood quarters. You probably have already started by saving at least one or more of each different kind. If you are like many other Americans, you may have a drawer or purse full of them already. This is a good start, but to get the most out of this new challenge you will have to go a bit further. Get those coins out and take a good look at them. There may be many things that you did not realize the first time you glanced at them.

There is something to be said for saving as many of the Statehood quarters as you can find, but keep in mind that in the future they may be the only kind of quarters that you will see in circulation. You will have to decide at some point if you want to become a hoarder, a speculator, or a collector. Whichever course you take will probably have some benefits, depending on how you approach your objective.

The government is making Statehood quarters in quantities sufficient to circulate them throughout the entire country. In most cases, this would ensure that they will be forever common and never worth much more than their face value. But that is not the way things are working out for the Statehood quarters. These coins are so popular that "everyone"

• • •

In addition to the coins that will be made for circulation at the mints in Philadelphia and Denver there will also be a special offering of Proof coins made for collectors at the San Francisco Mint. These coins are not intended for use in circulation and can only be obtained by purchasing them from the Mint, through a coin dealer, or from another collector. Proof coins are specimens of each design that are made as perfect examples of the highest quality of minting. They are made for museums and collectors, and because of the effort that goes into making them, they are not intended for use as money even though they have the same legal tender status as regular coins.

Proof coins made at the San Francisco Mint are identified by an s mintmark on the obverse at the right of the head. Two different kinds of Proof specimens are offered for sale to collectors. Normal Proofs are superb examples of coins that are made of the same composition as circulation coins. Special deluxe silver Proofs are also made for collectors. These are sold for an additional premium and are only made in limited quantities.

A complete set of Statehood quarters for each state thus consists of the following: One example from the Denver Mint, one from Philadelphia, one copper-nickel Proof, and one silver Proof. In numismatic parlance these are indicated as 1999-P, 1999-D, 1999-S Proof, and 1999-S silver Proof.

Proof coins can be purchased from the United States Mint only during the year of issue. The cost of a current set of five Statehood quarters is $13.95, but subject to change without notice. Information about availability and cost can be obtained by telephoning 1-800-USA-MINT. Other offerings from the mint can be found at their website, usmint.gov.

DELAWARE 1999

December 7, 1787 • "The First State"

The design on this coin depicts Caesar Rodney on Horseback, in the course of his historic 80-mile ride through the terrible summer's heat and thunderstorms to attend the meeting of the Continental Congress in 1776. He arrived at Independence Hall on the afternoon of July 2, during the last minute of the debate on independence, in time to cast his vote for independence.

Capital: Dover
Flower: Peach blossom
Tree: American holly
Bird: Blue hen chicken

As the first of the 13 original colonies to ratify the federal Constitution, on December 7, 1787, Delaware has the distinction of being the first U.S. state, an honor that is proudly proclaimed on the Delaware quarter.

1999-P 373,400,000; 1999-D 400,832,000; 1999-S Proof

PENNSYLVANIA 1999

December 12, 1787 • "The Keystone State"

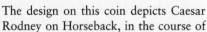

An outline of the state forms the background of this design that incorporates a keystone and an allegorical female figure known as Commonwealth. The state motto LIBERTY, INDEPENDENCE, VIRTUE is at the right side of the coin; the date of entry into statehood, 1787, is at the top.

Capital: Harrisburg
Flower: Mountain laurel
Tree: Hemlock
Bird: Ruffed grouse

The statue depicted is atop the Pennsylvania capitol dome. It is a bronze-gilded 14' 6" high female that has topped the capitol dome since 1905. Her right arm extends in mercy; her left arm grasps a ribbon mace to symbolize justice. The keystone is symbolic of Pennsylvania, known as the Keystone State.

1999-P 349,000,000; 1999-D 358,332,000; 1999-S Proof

NEW JERSEY 1999

December 18, 1787 • "The Garden State"

The design on the New Jersey quarter shows the famous scene of George Washington crossing the Delaware River, based on the 1851 painting by Emmanuel Leutze. It shows the Colonial Army on the way to victories against the British at the battles of Trenton and Princeton.

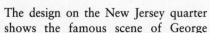

The words CROSSROADS OF THE REVOLUTION are beneath the scene. The original painting hangs in the Metropolitan Museum of Art in New York City.

Capital: Trenton
Flower: Purple violet
Tree: Red oak
Bird: Eastern goldfinch

New Jersey was the third of the original colonies to sign the Constitution. Coins for this state were first issued in March 1999.

1999-P 363,200,000; 1999-D 299,028,000; 1999-S Proof

GEORGIA 1999

January 2, 1788 • "The Empire State of the South"

A Georgia peach is featured prominently in the center of an outline of the state of Georgia. The fruit has long been associated with the state as a recognized symbol. The central design is bordered in live oak sprigs, symbolic of the state tree. Draped across the top of the design is a banner bearing the state motto, WISDOM, JUSTICE, MODERATION.

Capital: Atlanta
Flower: Cherokee rose
Tree: Live oak
Bird: Brown thrasher

Georgia entered the Union on January 2, 1788, as the fourth state. The first United States gold rush took place in Georgia, and Templeton Reid, a local jeweler, minted private gold coins there in 1830.

1999-P 451,188,000; 1999-D 488,744,000; 1999-S Proof

CONNECTICUT 1999

January 9, 1788 • "The Constitution State"

The famous Charter Oak tree is pictured on this coin. It is a reminder of the founding days of this colony. Connecticut had formed an independent colonial government under the terms of a charter granted by King Charles II in 1662. The charter was later challenged by King James II who, in 1687, demanded that it be surrendered to him.

In the middle of a discussion, with the charter on the table between opposing parties, candles were mysteriously snuffed out. When they were relighted, the charter was gone. Captain Joseph Wadsworth saved it from the British by hiding it in a white oak on the property of the Wyllys family.

Capital: Hartford
Flower: Mountain laurel
Tree: White oak
Bird: American robin

1999-P 688,744,000; 1999-D 658,489,000; 1999-S Proof

MASSACHUSETTS 2000

February 6, 1788 • "The Bay State"

The highly recognizable icon of the Colonial Minuteman was used as part of the motif in the design of the Massachusetts quarter. It commemorates battles at the towns of Lexington and Concord between British troops and rebellious colonists that sparked the fight for American independence from the British crown. The minuteman on this coin was adapted from sculptor Daniel Chester French's famous statue in Lexington.

Capital: Boston
Flower: Mayflower
Tree: American elm
Bird: Chickadee

In the background is an outline map of Massachusetts and in the right field are the words THE BAY STATE. The pilgrims settled in the Commonwealth of Massachusetts and celebrated the first Thanksgiving there.

2000-P; 2000-D; 2000-S Proof

MARYLAND 2000

April 28, 1788 • "The Old Line State"

The design on the Maryland quarter highlights the striking Maryland Statehouse surrounded by white oak leaf clusters on either side. The state's nickname, THE OLD LINE STATE, flanks the statehouse, a distinctive building dating back to 1772. It features the country's largest wooden dome built without nails. Besides housing Maryland's colonial legislature, it was also crucial to our national history. From 1783 to 1784, the Maryland Statehouse served as the nation's first peacetime capital.

Capital: Annapolis
Flower: Black-eyed susan
Tree: White oak
Bird: Baltimore oriole

The Treaty of Paris was ratified here, officially ending the Revolutionary War. A treasure preserved, the statehouse continues as the country's oldest state capital building still in legislative use.

2000-P; 2000-D; 2000-S Proof

SOUTH CAROLINA 2000

May 23, 1788 • "The Palmetto State"

An outline of the state forms the background for the design on South Carolina's commemorative quarter. It contains the words THE PALMETTO STATE and has a star indicating the location of its capital, Columbia. In the foreground is a palmetto tree on the right and a wren perched on a sprig of jessamine.

Capital: Columbia
Flower: Yellow jessamine
Tree: Palmetto
Bird: Carolina wren

More battles of the American Revolution took place in South Carolina than in any other state, and the first shots of the Civil War were fired in South Carolina. The Charleston Museum, opened in 1773, is the oldest in the United States.

2000-P; 2000-D; 2000-S Proof

NEW HAMPSHIRE 2000

June 21, 1788 • "The Granite State"

Concord

New Hampshire's "Old Man of the Mountain" is perhaps the state's most prominent and memorable landmark. The unusual rock formation is shown in profile as seen from Franconia Notch in the central part of the state. The state motto, LIVE FREE OR DIE, inscribed at the left side of the coin, dates back to the Revolutionary War and exemplifies the sentiment of this state for gaining independence.

Capital: Concord
Flower: Purple lilac
Tree: White birch
Bird: Purple finch

New Hampshire was the ninth state to enter the Union. A crescent of nine stars lines the right border in recognition of this event.

2000-P; 2000-D; 2000-S Proof

VIRGINIA 2000

June 25, 1788 • "The Old Dominion"   Richmond•

The Jamestown settlement in Virginia is commemorated on this quarter. The scene shows the first three ships landing and the inscription JAMESTOWN 1607–2007. The word beneath the waterline, QUADRICENTENNIAL, refers to the four-hundredth anniversary of the first permanent settlement in America, which will occur in the year 2007.

Capital: Richmond
Flower: Dogwood
Tree: Dogwood
Bird: Cardinal

Survivors of the first harsh winters were encouraged to stay by the arrival of new settlers and supplies in 1610. Two years later tobacco cultivation was started and the colony began to prosper. In 1619 the first representative assembly in America was held in Jamestown.

2000-P; 2000-D; 2000-S Proof

NEW YORK 2001

July 26, 1788 • "The Empire State"

Home to the largest city in the United States, New York offers many design possibilities for its state quarter. New York City was the nation's first capital, which could be commemorated with a depiction of the capitol building. Other themes for New York City, which has been called "The Gateway to Freedom," might be the Statue of Liberty, Ellis Island, the world-famous skyline, or the Empire State Building.

Other memorable icons of the state worthy of celebrating are the victory at Saratoga, Henry Hudson's exploration in his ship *Half Moon,* Fort Ticonderoga, and Niagara Falls.

Capital: *Albany*
Flower: *Rose*
Tree: *Sugar maple*
Bird: *Bluebird*

2001-P; 2001-D; 2001-S Proof

NORTH CAROLINA 2001

November 21, 1789 • "The Tar Heel State"

Capital: *Raleigh*
Flower: *Dogwood*
Tree: *Pine*
Bird: *Cardinal*

North Carolina, and in particular Kitty Hawk, is best remembered as the home of the Wright Brothers, who are credited with man's first controlled flight in a heavier-than-air machine. The Wright Brothers National Memorial is a popular attraction to the area, and some representation of this monumental event would be an ideal theme for this state's quarter.

A second and also very well recognized landmark is the famous lighthouse at Cape Hatteras. The Great Smoky Mountains National Park and its familiar landscape could also be remembered on these coins.

2001-P; 2001-D; 2001-S Proof

⌂Providence   RHODE ISLAND 2001

May 29, 1790 • "The Ocean State"

The smallest state in the Union is not without numerous suitable themes for its commemorative quarter. The most likely candidate is a representation of Roger Williams, founder of the city of Providence in 1635. Perhaps he will be shown arriving on the shore in a canoe and being greeted by Native Americans, as he was on a similar commemorative half dollar minted for the state in 1936.

Rhode Island is home to the oldest synagogue in the United States, Touro Synagogue, which was built in 1763 and is still standing in Newport. The bluffs and islands along this coastal state are familiar tourist attractions.

Capital: Providence
Flower: Violet
Tree: Red maple
Bird: Rhode Island red

2001-P; 2001-D; 2001-S Proof

VERMONT 2001

March 4, 1791 • "The Green Mountain State"

Montpelier

Vermont was not one of the original thirteen colonies that formed the United States. It joined the union in 1791 and became the fourteenth state. The role of the Green Mountain Boys in the Revolutionary War, the Battle of Bennington, or a depiction of Ira Allen, founder of the state, would make ideal subjects for this commemorative quarter.

Capital: Montpelier
Flower: Red clover
Tree: Sugar maple
Bird: Hermit thrush

In 1777 Vermont passed the first constitution to prohibit slavery and to allow all men to vote. The state is also famous for its marble quarries, maple syrup, dairy products, and majestic scenery.

2001-P; 2001-D; 2001-S Proof

KENTUCKY 2001

June 1, 1792 • "The Bluegrass State"

As the fifteenth state to join the Union, Kentucky has already been recognized on a quarter as long ago as 1796. The very first American quarters displayed the head of Liberty within an arrangement of 15 stars that were meant to represent each of the states. With the growth of the nation that custom was abandoned and only 13 stars were used on most subsequent coins.

Abraham Lincoln was born in Kentucky in 1709. His birthplace might well be remembered on this state's commemorative coin. Another famous son was Daniel Boone, the frontiersman who established a peaceful relationship with Chief Black Fish.

Capital: Frankfort
Flower: Goldenrod
Tree: Tulip poplar
Bird: Cardinal

2001-P; 2001-D; 2001-S Proof

TENNESSEE 2002

June 1, 1796 • "The Volunteer State"

Capital: Nashville
Flower: Iris
Tree: Tulip poplar
Bird: Mockingbird

The Great Smoky Mountains National Park may be one of the sites memorialized on Tennessee's Statehood quarter. Other possibilities are the Hermitage, home of President Andrew Jackson, near Nashville; or even the Grand Ole Opry and Opryland USA theme park, which is one of the best-known attractions in the state that is beloved by millions as the country music capital of the world.

The state is rich with Civil War battle sites that are of interest to all visitors, although Graceland, the home of entertainer Elvis Presley in Memphis, is probably of equal popularity.

2002-P; 2002-D; 2002-S Proof

OHIO 2002

March 1, 1803 • "The Buckeye State"

Artists will have a plethora of topics to choose from in selecting a theme for the Ohio commemorative quarter. Seven American presidents were born in Ohio, and any or all of them could be portrayed on these coins. The list is composed of Garfield, Grant, Harding, Benjamin Harrison, Hayes, McKinley, and Taft. Ohio was also the home of the first professional baseball team, the Cincinnati Red Stockings.

Capital: Columbus
Flower: Scarlet carnation
Tree: Buckeye
Bird: Cardinal

The Mound City Group National Monuments and Indian burial mounds are well-known landmarks, as is the Cedar Point and King's Island amusement parks and the Neil Armstrong Air and Space Museum.

2002-P; 2002-D; 2002-S Proof

LOUISIANA 2002

April 30, 1812 • "The Pelican State"   Baton Rouge

It is almost certain that a pelican will appear somewhere on the coin of the state that honors it as its state bird. Of equal importance, and a likely subject, is the Mardi Gras festival that is held in New Orleans each year. The city is known worldwide for its jazz and the colorful celebration that is part of the area's culture.

Capital: Baton Rouge
Flower: Magnolia
Tree: Cypress
Bird: Eastern brown pelican

Louisiana is also home to the busiest port in the United States, and it is the second biggest mining state after Alaska. The French Quarter of New Orleans and the Jean Lafitte National Historical Park are two attractions that could also be remembered.

2002-P; 2002-D; 2002-S Proof

INDIANA 2002

Indianapolis

December 11, 1816 • "The Hoosier State"

Indianapolis, the largest and best-known city in Indiana, is home to the famous Indianapolis 500 auto race that is held each year at its world renowned track. The state is also distinguished by its Children's Museum in Indianapolis and the Conner Prarie Pioneer Settlement in Noiblesville. The Lincoln Boyhood Memorial in Lincoln City may well be one of the attractions most likely to be honored on this state's coin.

Capital: Indianapolis
Flower: Peony
Tree: Tulip poplar
Bird: Cardinal

Indiana's famous Lost River will probably not be shown on these quarters because it travels 22 miles underground, but chances are you will see a race car somewhere.

1999-P; 1999-D; 2002-S Proof

MISSISSIPPI 2002

December 10, 1817 • "The Magnolia State"

Jackson

Capital: Jackson
Flower: Magnolia
Tree: Magnolia
Bird: Mockingbird

It is a safe bet that Mississippi will depict a magnolia somewhere on its State-hood quarter. There are, of course, many remarkable events and people that can be commemorated. Jefferson Davis, president of the Confederate States of America, was born in Mississippi, and may well be remembered on this coin. Mississippi is also well known as the first state to celebrate Memorial Day, which was originally called Decoration Day. The first state-run college for women was opened in Columbus in 1884.

The Old Capitol at Jackson and the Old Spanish Fort at Pascagoula are probably the leading contenders to be shown on these coins.

2002-P; 2002-D; 2002-S Proof

ILLINOIS 2003

December 3, 1818 • "The Prairie State"

Abraham Lincoln lived and worked in Illinois, and he is buried there. As one of the state's favorite sons, he is almost certain to be remembered in some way on the quarter dedicated to Illinois. Lincoln has been commemorated on many other American coins and paper money. His image on the current one-cent coin is well known throughout the world.

Capital: Springfield
Flower: Native violet
Tree: White oak
Bird: Cardinal

Other Illinois landmarks include Lincoln's home and tomb; Chicago's Sears Tower, one of the tallest buildings in the world; and the O'Hare airport, one of the busiest airports in the world.

2003-P; 2003-D; 2003-S Proof

ALABAMA 2003

December 14, 1819 • "The Camellia State"

Capital: Montgomery
Flower: Camellia
Tree: Southern longleaf pine
Bird: Yellowhammer

Montgomery, Alabama, was selected to be the state capital of the Confederate States of America in 1861, and it is quite possible that some reference to that may be shown on this state's quarter. The state flower, the camellia, will no doubt also be included for identification of what is known as the Camellia State. A belated commemorative half dollar was made for this state in 1921 recognizing the bicentennial of the 22nd state.

Alabama is a major center for rocket and space research, and these coins may also recognize that industry and the Alabama Space and Rocket Center in Huntsville.

2003-P; 2003-D; 2003-S Proof

MAINE 2003

March 15, 1820 • "The Pine Tree State"

Augusta

The centennial of Maine's entry into the Union was celebrated in 1920 with the issue of a commemorative half dollar. That coin, considered one of the most artistic of all commemorative pieces, displays the coat of arms of the state on the obverse and a legend within a wreath on the reverse. Perhaps the new Statehood quarter will surpass the old commemorative with something done in remembrance of Maine's rocky seacoast, fishing villages, and delicious lobster.

Mount Katahdin, a likely subject for the quarter, is the highest spot in Maine and the first place in the continental United States that the sun hits in the morning.

Capital: Augusta
*Flower: White pine cone
    and tassel*
Tree: Eastern white pine
Bird: Chickadee

2003-P; 2003-D; 2003-S Proof

MISSOURI 2003

August 10, 1821 • "The Show Me State" Jefferson City

Capital: Jefferson City
Flower: Hawthorn
Tree: Dogwood
Bird: Bluebird

It will not be difficult to select something to serve as a recognizable symbol for this great state. The Gateway Arch in St. Louis is a likely candidate. At 630 feet it is the tallest monument in the United States and is familiar to all. Missouri is also not without its share of famous people who could represent the state. President Harry S Truman is perhaps the leading contender. Others include agricultural scientist George Washington Carver and author Mark Twain.

The state is known as the gateway to the West and will be remembered for its importance as a shipping center both past and present.

2003-P; 2003-D; 2003-S Proof

ARKANSAS 2003

June 15, 1836 • "The Natural State"

Little Rock

Arkansas is famous for its tourist attractions in Hot Springs National Park and the Fort Smith National Historic Site. The state has the only working diamond mine in North America and is a mecca for those who would explore the area. A native son from Little Rock, Matt Rothert, was the person responsible for adding the motto IN GOD WE TRUST to United States paper money. A second numismatic attraction in the state is the Gallery Mint Museum in Eureka Springs.

Capital: Little Rock
Flower: Apple blossom
Tree: Pine
Bird: Mockingbird

President Bill Clinton was born in Arkansas and served as one of its governors.

2003-P; 2003-D; 2003-S Proof

MICHIGAN 2004

January 26, 1837 • "The Wolverine State"

Lansing

Detroit, the Motor City, will quite likely be recognized in one form or another on this state's commemorative coins. Automobiles are one of the state's most important products. Dearborn is the home of Greenfield Village and the Henry Ford Museum. The state is also well known for its many lakes, including Lake Michigan, which is the largest lake lying entirely in the United States.

Capital: Lansing
Flower: Apple blossom
Tree: White pine
Bird: Robin

In 1837 Michigan was the 26th state to enter the Union, and the last to be so honored until Florida joined as the 27th state eight years later in 1845.

2004-P; 2004-D; 2004-S Proof

FLORIDA 2004

•Tallahassee

March 3, 1845 • "The Sunshine State"

People from all over the world enjoy Florida's sunny climate and tourist attractions. Kennedy Space Center in Cape Canaveral might well be one of the elements remembered in the design of this state's quarter. Other places of interest include Disney World and Universal Studios near Orlando, Sea World, and Everglades National Park. The entire state is a haven for the visitors and retired who enjoy its nearly ideal weather.

St. Augustine, the oldest permanent European settlement in the United States, is almost certain to be the most popular choice for commemoration.

Capital: Tallahassee
Flower: Orange blossom
Tree: Sabal palmetto palm
Bird: Mockingbird

2004-P; 2004-D; 2004-S Proof

TEXAS 2004

December 9, 1845 • "The Lone Star State"

Austin

The state of Texas has already been honored on a United States commemorative half dollar that was minted from 1934 to 1938. That attractive coin featured a large star and eagle on the obverse and portraits of General Sam Houston and Stephen Austin, founders of the Republic and State of Texas, on the reverse. These are important figures in the history of the state who might well be again remembered on the new Statehood quarter.

Capital: Austin
Flower: Bluebonnet
Tree: Pecan
Bird: Mockingbird

Second only to the founders in popularity is the Alamo in San Antonio. President Lyndon Johnson National Historic Site could also be cited in tribute to the state's famous president.

2004-P; 2004-D; 2004-S Proof

IOWA 2004

Des Moines

December 28, 1846 • "The Hawkeye State"

The Iowa state capitol building at Iowa City, the first stone capitol in the country, would be an ideal monument for this state's commemorative quarter. Iowa is also rich in other suitable subjects. The bridge built in 1856 between Davenport and Rock Island was the first bridge to span the Mississippi River. Herbert Hoover was born in West Branch, and Buffalo Bill Cody, who was a frontiersman and the head of a famous Wild West show, was also born in Iowa.

Visitors to the state are probably most familiar with the Living History Farms in Des Moines and the Amana Colonies.

Capital: Des Moines
Flower: Wild rose
Tree: Oak
Bird: Eastern goldfinch

2004-P; 2004-D; 2004-S Proof

WISCONSIN 2004

May 29, 1848 • "The Badger State"

Madison

Capital: Madison
Flower: Wood violet
Tree: Sugar maple
Bird: Robin

Do not expect to see a badger on this state's quarter. The term does not refer to the animal, but rather to the miners who often worked in tunnels in the formative years of the state. It seems more likely that the icon for this state will have something to do with its fame as a dairy state. Other possibilities are its ancient burial mounds near Blue Mounds.

The first kindergarten in America was opened in Milwaukee, Wisconsin, in 1865. It got its name from German immigrants who populated the city in its early years.

2004-P; 2004-D; 2004-S Proof

CALIFORNIA 2005

September 9, 1850 • "The Golden State"

The well-known California grizzly bear would be a very appropriate emblem for this state's commemorative coin. Equally recognizable is the San Francisco Bay Bridge, and scenes from Disneyland in San Diego. The most famous event in the history of this state is the discovery of gold in 1848 and the gold rush that it started. A miner panning for gold would be symbolic of the event and a likely candidate for inclusion in this statehood design.

Yosemite Valley, Lake Tahoe, Hollywood, and Sequoia National Park are all recognizable landmarks that could have a place on this quarter.

Capital: Sacramento
Flower: Golden poppy
Tree: California redwood
Bird: California valley quail

2005-P; 2005-D; 2005-S Proof

MINNESOTA 2005

May 11, 1858 • "The North Star State"

Minnesota entered the Union in 1858 as the 32nd state. It is famous for its many waterways and is called the Land of 10,000 Lakes, which is a miscalculation because the state actually has more than 15,000 lakes. One of the northernmost states, Minnesota is also the coldest contiguous state, second only to Alaska. For obvious reasons it is home to the United States Hockey Hall of Fame in Eveleth.

The North Star State, also sometimes called the Gopher State, is famous for Fort Snelling, Voyageurs National Park, and the Grand Portage National Monument.

Capital: St. Paul
Flower: Pink and white lady's slipper
Tree: Red pine
Bird: Common loon

2005-P; 2005-D; 2005-S Proof

OREGON 2005

•Salem

February 14, 1859 • "The Beaver State"

Oregon once had a coinage of its own when the gold-rich state established a mint in Oregon City to strike coins. In 1849 the legislature passed an act providing for five- and ten-dollar gold coins to be made from native ore. At the time this act was passed, Oregon had recently been made a United States territory by act of Congress. When the new governor arrived he declared the coinage unconstitutional and halted operations. A beaver was used as the principle design on these pieces.

It seems likely that a beaver will once again grace this state's commemorative coin in 2005.

Capital: Salem
Flower: Oregon grape
Tree: Douglas fir
Bird: Western meadowlark

2005-P; 2005-D; 2005-S Proof

KANSAS 2005

Topeka•

January 29, 1861 • "The Sunflower State"

Capital: Topeka
Flower: Native sunflower
Tree: Cottonwood
Bird: Western meadowlark

The home of President Dwight D. Eisenhower will without doubt want to honor its most famous citizen on the special quarter that is dedicated to Kansas in 2005. The state is also home to the Kansas Cosmosphere and Space Discovery Center in Hutchinson, as well as Fort Scott and Fort Larned national historical sites. Dodge City is a famous attraction that could also be remembered on this state's coin.

Kansas is the crossroads of the nation because of its location in the geographical center of the United States. It is one of the two biggest wheat-growing states in the country.

2005-P; 2005-D; 2005-S Proof

WEST VIRGINIA 2005

June 20, 1863 • "The Mountain State"

Charleston

West Virginia got its name from the people of western Virginia who formed their own government in 1861 during the Civil War. They petitioned to join the Union and were made a state in 1863. West Virginia is famous for the historical battlefield sites of Harpers Ferry, and Grave Creek Mound in Moundsville. The Monogahela National Forest and the state's mountain scenery and mineral springs are among its many fine attractions.

The coal mining industry, so important to the nation's economy, could be honored on this state's commemorative coin as a tribute to its many dedicated workers.

Capital: Charleston
Flower: Big rhododendron
Tree: Sugar maple
Bird: Cardinal

2005-P; 2005-D; 2005-S Proof

NEVADA 2006

October 31, 1864 • "The Silver State"

•Carson City

The United States Mint in Carson City once made coins from local silver and shipped them all over the country. The Mint was in operation from 1870 to 1893. Now Nevada will have a coin of its own in the form of a Statehood quarter. Perhaps the old Mint building will be used as an icon of the silver-producing state on the new coin. Both gold and silver were once plentiful in the Silver State, but today the biggest attractions are gaming establishments in Los Vegas, Reno, and Lake Tahoe.

Nevada is a Spanish term meaning "snow-covered," originally applied to the Sierra Nevada Mountains.

Capital: Carson City
Flower: Sagebrush
Tree: Single-leaf piñon and
  bristlecone pine
Bird: Mountain bluebird

2006-P; 2006-D; 2006-S Proof

NEBRASKA 2006

March 1, 1867 • "The Cornhusker State"

Expect to see an ear of corn on this state's coin. The nickname comes from the state's college football team, the University of Nebraska Cornhuskers. Nebraska is an important cattle state, the biggest meatpacking center in the world, and an important farm center worthy of recognition on the new quarter. The original territory was part of the Louisiana Purchase of 1803, and the scene of fur-trading activities prior to settlement in 1823.

Capital: Lincoln
Flower: Goldenrod
Tree: Cottonwood
Bird: Western meadowlark

The Oregon Trail is another landmark that may be noted on these coins, and some will propose that Boys Town should be honored for all it has done in the field of rehabilitation.

2006-P; 2006-D; 2006-S Proof

COLORADO 2006

August 1, 1876 • "The Centennial State"

Denver

Capital: Denver
Flower: Rocky Mountain
  columbine
Tree: Colorado blue spruce
Bird: Lark bunting

Colorado's capital city, Denver, is home to the United States Mint that will be producing some of the coins that will honor this state. The design they will use may reflect the state's beautiful scenery, in particular the famed Pikes Peak mountain. Colorado is home to more mountains over 14,000 feet than any other state and also boasts the world's highest bridge at 1,053 feet. Old mining towns and national parks contribute to the scenic interest of the state where "America the Beautiful" was composed.

The United States Air Force Academy and North American Aerospace Defense Command facilities are nationally known icons.

2006-P; 2006-D; 2006-S Proof

NORTH DAKOTA 2006

Bismarck

November 2, 1889 • "The Peace Garden State"

The United States acquired North Dakota in the Louisiana Purchase of 1803. Fur trade dominated the territory for over half a century before settlers arrived in the 1860s. North Dakota became the nation's 39th state in 1889. It derives its name from a Sioux Indian word meaning "friend." One of the border states with Canada, North Dakota is famous as one of the two biggest wheat-growing states, and for its other farm products.

Capital: Bismarck
Flower: Wild prairie rose
Tree: American elm
Bird: Western meadowlark

Theodore Roosevelt was a rancher in North Dakota before he became president and will probably be remembered on the Statehood quarter of this state.

2006-P; 2006-D; 2006-S Proof

SOUTH DAKOTA 2006

•Pierre

November 2, 1889 • "The Coyote State"

Capital: Pierre
Flower: Pasqueflower
Tree: Black Hills spruce
Bird: Chinese ring-necked
  pheasant

One can almost predict with certainty that the outstanding Mount Rushmore National Memorial will be shown somewhere on the commemorative quarter of this state. The famous mountain carving depicting Presidents Washington, Jefferson, Lincoln, and Theodore Roosevelt created by artist Gutzon Borglum are considered a national treasure. Some other almost equally interesting candidates include Wounded Knee Battlefield, Crazy Horse, Sitting Bull, and Wild Bill Hickok.

Home of the Black Hills and Badlands, the state is known for mining (gold, silver, and feldspar), farmland, and for its rich heritage as the Land of the Sioux Indians.

2006-P; 2006-D; 2006-S Proof

MONTANA 2007

•Helena

November 8, 1889 • "The Treasure State"

Montana gets its state name from a Spanish word meaning "mountainous." It is the fourth largest state after Alaska, Texas, and California. The most famous Indian battle in the history of the nation, where General Custer lost his life, took place in Montana at Little Bighorn in 1876. The Little Bighorn National Monument in Crow Agency is an important tourist attraction, as is the Museum of the Rockies in Bozeman.

Capital: Helena
Flower: Bitterroot
Tree: Ponderosa pine
Bird: Western meadowlark

Some of the state's familiar scenery could be shown on their commemorative quarter in recognition of its very beautiful national parks.

2007-P; 2007-D; 2007-S Proof

WASHINGTON 2007

November 11, 1889 • "The Evergreen State"

•Olympia

Capital: Olympia
Flower: Western
  rhododendron
Tree: Western hemlock
Bird: Willow goldfinch

The early history of Washington centered around the fur trade. It became a territory in 1853 and was admitted to the Union in 1889. The development of power on the Columbia River from the Grand Coulee Dam and Bonneville Dam enabled the region to become one of the country's great industrial centers. The Grand Coulee is the largest concrete dam in the world and a likely candidate for the state's icon.

Mount Rainier, noted for its beauty and volcanic activity, is a major attraction to the area and might also be shown on this state's coin, along with the famous Space Needle of Seattle.

2007-P; 2007-D; 2007-S Proof

IDAHO 2007

July 3, 1890 • "The Gem State"

The Lewis and Clark expedition of 1805 preceded the activities of Canadian and American fur traders who worked this region. Franklin was the first permanent settlement in 1860, and the discovery of gold that year led to a rapid expansion. Idaho Territory was established in 1863, but Indian troubles continued until late 1870s. Idaho became a state in 1890. The first hydroelectric power plant built by the federal government was the Minidoka Dam on the Snake River in 1909.

Capital: Boise
Flower: Syringa
Tree: White pine
Bird: Mountain bluebird

If a potato appears on this state's coin it will achieve well-deserved recognition. Two-thirds of all potatoes grown in the United States come from this state.

2007-P; 2007-D; 2007-S Proof

WYOMING 2007

July 10, 1890 • "The Equality State"

Wyoming is the home of Yellowstone National Park and the tallest active geyser, Steamboat Geyser, which could be one of the choices for a recognizable image on this Statehood coin. Yellowstone, established in 1872, and Grand Teton national parks are both popular tourist attractions, as are Fort Laramie and the Buffalo Bill Historical Center in Cody.

Capital: Cheyenne
Flower: Indian paintbrush
Tree: Plains cottonwood
Bird: Western meadowlark

Early development of this area was linked to the fur trade and westward migration. Fur trading posts were established at Fort Laramie and Fort Bridger. Indian wars of the 1860s failed to stem immigration to this fertile land, which became a state in 1890.

2007-P; 2007-D; 2007-S Proof

UTAH 2007

Salt Lake City   January 4, 1896 • "The Beehive State"

Rainbow Bridge in Utah is the largest natural arch or rock bridge in the world, and a possible candidate for inclusion on this state's quarter. Other images might be the Indian cliff dwellings or Temple Square, home of the Mormon Church headquarters in Salt Lake City. The very familiar Great Salt Lake, however, could hardly be depicted on a coin.

When the Mormons first settled this area in 1850, they found quantities of gold, which they made into coins for their use in trade. One of them included a beehive in its design as an appropriate symbol of the Beehive State.

Capital: Salt Lake City
Flower: Sego lily
Tree: Blue spruce
Bird: Seagull

2007-P; 2007-D; 2007-S Proof

OKLAHOMA 2008

November 16, 1907 • "The Sooner State"   Oklahoma City

Oklahoma, part of the Louisiana Purchase of 1803, was known as Indian Territory (though not made a territorial government) after it became the home of the "Five Civilized Tribes" in 1828–1847. As white settlers pressed west, land was opened for homesteading, and the area became a state in 1907. Today Oklahoma is populated by more Native Americans than any other state. Honoring their heritage would be an ideal subject for this state's quarter.

Famous Oklahomans worth remembering include Will Rogers, Maria Tallchief, Jim Thorpe, Mickey Mantle, Carry Nation, Wiley Post, and General Patrick J. Hurley.

Capital: Oklahoma City
Flower: Mistletoe
Tree: Redbud
Bird: Scissor-tailed
  flycatcher

2008-P; 2008-D; 2008-S Proof

NEW MEXICO 2008

January 6, 1912 • "Land of Enchantment"

It seems doubtful that the roadrunner would appear on this state's coin, but that would be an interesting change from other state designs. The lovely yucca flower might seem a better choice to many, and there is no shortage of famous people who could be recognized. Kit Carson would probably lead the list, followed closely by Billy the Kid and Archbishop Jean Baptiste Lamy.

Franciscan Marcos de Niza and a former slave named Estevanico explored the area in 1539 seeking gold. The first European settlements were at San Juan Pueblo in 1598 and Santa Fe in 1610. Early settlers struggled with Apaches, Comanches, Navajos and Mexicans before achieving statehood in 1912.

Capital: Santa Fe
Flower: Yucca
Tree: Piñon
Bird: Roadrunner

2008-P; 2008-D; 2008-S Proof

ARIZONA 2008

February 14, 1912 • "The Grand Canyon State"

A state as scenic as Arizona will have many subjects to choose from in selecting a theme for their Statehood coin. The first choice may be the Grand Canyon. The Grand Canyon is the largest land gorge in the world and one of the world's natural wonders. The Painted Desert, Petrified Forest, or Hoover Dam could be alternate choices.

The Spanish first came to the area in 1549. Eusebio Francisco Kino established missions there in 1690. It became a part of the United States by the Treaty of Guadalupe Hidalgo in 1848, and was made a territory in 1863.

Capital: Phoenix
Flower: Saguaro cactus blossom
Tree: Paloverde
Bird: Cactus wren

2008-P; 2008-D; 2008-S Proof

ALASKA 2008

Juneau

January 3, 1959 • "The Last Frontier"

As the largest and coldest state in the union, Alaska will find many things to put on their coin. A good choice would be to pay tribute to Secretary of State W. H. Seward, who was instrumental in purchasing the territory from Russia in 1867 for $7.2 million. Denali National Park, Mendenhall Glacier, and Mount McKinley are also recognizable attractions that could be used.

Alaska has the distinction of already having had special tokens made for use there as early as 1935. These were issued by the government for use by the colonists of the Matanuska Valley Colonization Project to supply federal aid.

Capital: Juneau
Flower: Forget-me-not
Tree: Sitka spruce
Bird: Willow ptarmigan

2008-P; 2008-D; 2008-S Proof

HAWAII 2008

Honolulu

August 21, 1959 • "The Aloha State"

Most people will recognize Hawaii by the outline of its most famous mountain, Diamond Head, which overshadows Waikiki Beach in Honolulu. This might well be incorporated into the design on this Statehood quarter. A second choice would be the U.S.S. *Arizona* Memorial at Pearl Harbor. The state's many volcanoes, waterfalls, and lush vegetation offer much to commemorate.

Capital: Honolulu
Flower: Yellow hibiscus
Tree: Kukui (candlenut)
Bird: Hawaiian goose

Hawaii is the only state made up entirely of islands. Of the 122 land masses in the group, only 7 of them are inhabited. Hawaii's Mauna Loa is the biggest active volcano in the United States.

2008-P; 2008-D; 2008-S Proof

4

Designing the 50 State Quarters™

Now that you have seen some of the new Statehood quarters and have some idea of what others could look like when they are made in the future, you may have thoughts of your own about what the quarter of your state should look like. If so, you are reacting exactly the way the originators of this program anticipated.

Very few people ever get the chance to design a real coin for circulation. The designs have been changed infrequently in the past and Mint artists are usually assigned to do the work required on any new issues. This time, however, the rules have been changed, and people across the country have an opportunity to be part of the design process. You too can participate in this exciting process if you have the talent, imagination, and initiative to do so.

Suggesting a theme or a design for your state's quarter is not a complicated process, but the rules for going about it do vary from state to state, as one would expect of a program intended to express the individuality of each state. The governor of each state, therefore, is responsible for deciding how his or her state's design choice will be made.

Some states will make their selections through a committee rather than opening the process to the general public. Others are seeking opinions from everyone—including even the youngest schoolchildren.

If you have a desire to participate in proposing a design for the 50 State Quarters program, there are guidelines you will have to follow. Some requirements will also have to be met in order to make all of the state quarters part of a homogeneous series of national coins. The first requisites to explore are how the governor of your state intends to conduct the program. Other requirements and some suggestions for how to proceed are presented in this chapter.

A standard format will be used for all coins in the 50 State Quarters program. State designs are displayed only on the reverse side of the quarters. Designing, collecting, and enjoying this new group of coins is an opportunity that should not be passed by. When other events that marked the entry into the new millennium are forgotten, the designs on these coins will still be around to remind us that we have entered a new age. Millennium coinage, like the Roman coins of old, will endure for many future generations.

Could your ideas be good enough for use on a circulating American coin? Of course. Anything representative of your state, and in good taste, would be appropriate. In past years some of the most successful designs used on our nation's coins were simple but meaningful. Take, for instance, the lovely head of Liberty engraved by Mint Designer Charles Barber in 1892.

The ancient Roman silver denarius *was nearly the same size and weight as a United States dime. Some of the designs were even very similar to those on modern coins. Compare the U.S. Barber dime of 1904 with the Roman* denarius *of Augustus, minted in* A.D. *14. Both have a classic and timeless design.*

State designs are submitted and selected through a process determined by the governor of each state. The Mint reviews the designs for coinability before each governor selects a final design. During the process, review committees may make comments and suggestions as to the appropriateness of each design.

In an example of how one state's program worked, Tennessee Governor Don Sundquist appointed a citizens committee to solicit, review, and recommend to him possible designs for their state quarter. A chairman was selected to head the group, and plans were made to reach out to the general public for a broad range of ideas. Tennessee students and artists were all invited to submit concepts and suggestions.

Suggestions submitted to a governor may be forwarded to the Mint as theme recommendations or as drawings. Mint artists then prepare comprehensive and functional artwork for approval by the governor.

THE COIN DESIGN PROCESS

State quarter designs will be selected and approved by the process established by Secretary of the Treasury Robert E. Rubin on January 9, 1998, in accordance with Public Law 105-124. In this process, governors are invited to submit design ideas or graphics. Drawings of the various concepts will be reviewed by the Mint, the Citizens Commemorative Coin Advisory Committee, and the Fine Arts Commission. They will then be sent to the Secretary of the Treasury for final review and approval. The Secretary of the Treasury will select between three and five candidate designs that will be forwarded to the state governor's office for final selection through a process determined by the governor. Finally, the Secretary of the Treasury will give the final approval to the selected design for each state.

The Citizens Commemorative Coin Advisory Committee was established by Act of Congress, Public Law 102-390, to pass judgment on the appropriateness of all commemorative coin designs. The committee advises Congress on commemorative coin themes, mintage levels, and years of issue, and advises the Secretary of the Treasury on commemorative coin designs. It is composed of seven members: three from the numismatic community, three from the general public, and one from the U.S. Mint. A member of the Commission of Fine Arts may participate as a non-voting member. Each of the 50 Statehood quarters designs is reviewed by this committee prior to being returned to a governor.

The United States Commission of Fine Arts was established by Congress as an independent agency in 1910 to advise the government on matters of art and architecture that affect the appearance of the nation's capital. The President appoints seven members for four-year terms. The Commission also advises the U.S. Mint on the designs of coins and medals and is responsible for advising the President or Congressional committees on questions of art.

All current inscriptions will appear on the new quarters. The 50 States Commemorative Coin Program Act did not affect the current statutory requirement that United States coins shall have the inscriptions IN GOD WE TRUST, LIBERTY, UNITED STATES OF AMERICA, E PLURIBUS UNUM, and a designation of the value of the coin and the year of minting or issuance. Three of the inscriptions (UNITED STATES OF AMERICA, E PLURIBUS UNUM, and a designation of value) are required to be placed on the reverse of each coin. However, on May 29, 1998, the President signed Public Law 105-176, which allows for any inscription or inscriptions currently required on the reverse of the quarter to be repositioned on the obverse of the new quarters. This law was enacted to provide for greater creative flexibility in developing the state designs.

GUIDELINES FOR THE 50 STATE DESIGNS

The 50 State Quarters Program Act provides for designs to be submitted in accordance with the design selection and approval process developed by and in sole discretion of the Secretary of the Treasury. It is important that the nation's coinage and currency bear dignified designs of which the citizens of the United States can be proud. The Act further requires that the Secretary shall not select any frivolous or inappropriate designs; no head-and-shoulders portrait or bust of any person, living or dead, and no portrait of a living person may be included in the design.

All designs must maintain a dignity befitting the nation's coinage, and shall have broad appeal to the citizens of the state and avoid controversial subjects or symbols that are likely to offend.

Suitable subject matter for design concepts include state landmarks (natural and man-made), landscapes, historically significant buildings, symbols of state resources or industries, official state flora and fauna, state icons (e.g., Texas Lone Star, Wyoming bronco, etc.), and outlines of states. No inscriptions should be included in the state design concept. State flags and seals are not considered suitable.

Consistent with the authorizing legislation, the states are encouraged to submit concepts that promote the diffusion of knowledge among the youth of the United States about the state, its history and geography, and the rich diversity of our national heritage.

Priority consideration will be given to designs and concepts that are enduring representations of the state. Coins have a commercial life span of at least 30 years and are collected for generations.

Inappropriate design concepts include, but are not limited to, logos or depictions of specific commercial ventures, or private, educational, civic, religious, sports, or other organizations whose membership or ownership is not universal.

Concepts or background materials submitted to the Mint that are covered by copyright, trademark, or other rights (such as privacy and publicity rights) must include a release acceptable to the Mint from the rights owner. This release must allow the concept or materials to be used on the coin, in marketing and promotional materials, and on the Mint's website for unlimited worldwide distribution without change or restriction.

SELECTING THE DESIGNS

Stage 1. The Mint contacts each state governor approximately 18 months prior to the beginning of the year in which the state will be honored to initiate the state design process. The governor then appoints an individual from the state to serve as the Mint's liaison for the program.

Stage 2. The state then selects and provides to the Mint a minimum of three and a maximum of five design concepts or themes emblematic of the state. The process for identifying concepts will be one of the governor's choosing. Concepts should be provided to the Mint, accompanied by supporting material as appropriate—for example, photographs or sketches of landmarks, landscapes, and historical buildings, or official depictions of state symbols.

Stage 3. The Mint reviews concepts for appropriateness and coinability. If fewer than three concepts are submitted, the Mint will develop additional concepts as necessary.

Stage 4. The Mint produces drawings of all design concepts.

Stage 5. The Citizens Commemorative Coin Advisory Committee reviews drawings and recommends candidate designs.

Stage 6. The U.S. Fine Arts Commission reviews candidate designs.

Stage 7. Candidate designs are presented to the Secretary of the Treasury for review and approval.

Stage 8. The Mint returns approved designs to the governor for selection of the state design.

Stage 9. The state selects the final design through a process determined by the governor, within a time frame specified by the Mint.

Stage 10. The final design is returned to Treasury for Approval by the Secretary or his designee and forwarded to the Mint for production.

A LOOK AT THE PAST

Anyone who longs to design one of the Statehood quarters would do well to study America's past efforts at producing commemorative coins. Some of them are memorials to the very same states that will be honored with the new coins; others pay tribute to famous statesmen or events in our nation's past.

The United States Mint has been making commemorative coins since 1892. In the early years production was rather limited and sporadic. The coins almost never entered circulation, and few people ever got the chance to see one. With very few exceptions all of the commemorative coins made in the past were sold at a premium by agencies, or the government, to collectors and people who wanted to save them as souvenirs.

In 1986 the Statue of Liberty was commemorated on a half dollar that showed the statue against the New York skyline. Another modern commemorative, made in 1991, depicts the famous four presidents of the Mount Rushmore National Memorial.

Talented artists designed many of the commemorative coins of the past. Some of them are considered to be among our most beautiful coins, but unfortunately they never got into circulation and their artistry has been wasted or lost. By reinventing the commemorative coin program in the form of the 50 State Quarters program the government hopes to bring to the public a new appreciation of medallic artistry and interest in the history and grandeur of America.

Classic commemorative half-dollar coins of the past show a variety of styles and themes. The 1920 Maine Centennial coin would not be an acceptable design for a Statehood quarter because it reproduces the state's coat of arms. The California Diamond Jubilee half dollar has an ideal design showing a miner panning for gold.

Not all of the Statehood commemoratives of the past have been special coin designs. The very first attempt to pay tribute to the states came with the earliest American coins, when a decision was made to honor each state with a star or some symbol in the design. The first coin ever made at the Mint was a one-cent piece dated 1793. That coin had on the reverse a chain of 15 links symbolizing the unity of the states. Later coins had an arrangement of 15, 16, or 17 stars indicating additional states. From 1800 to the present most American coins have only 13 stars to honor the original founders. Some exceptions are the twenty-dollar gold pieces of 1907 to 1911 with 46 stars, and from 1912 to 1933 with 48 stars. The Sacagawea dollar begun in 2000 has 17 stars to honor the states at the time of the Louis and Clark expedition.

The Mint is still making commemorative coins, other than the Statehood pieces, in denominations of fifty cents, one dollar, five dollars, and ten dollars. These are not all made every year. The most popular coins seem to be the silver dollars. Modern commemorative coins are made in Proof and Uncirculated sets. They are part of an ongoing program to honor special people, places, and events in this unique way. Coin collectors, or anyone

America's first Statehood coin, the 1793 Chain cent, has an arrangement of fifteen links on the reverse showing the unity of all states. In 1796 the half dollar had sixteen stars to mark the addition of Tennessee into the Union.

interested in obtaining any of the current issues on commemorative coins, can order them directly from the United States Mint during the year of issue. Premiums generally range from about $10 to $250 depending on the denomination. Information about any of the Mint's current offerings can be obtained from their website at usmint.gov.

The 1935 Texas commemorative uses a star and an eagle to identify this state. In 1936 Rhode Island celebrated its tercentenary with a design showing Roger Williams, founder of the city of Providence, arriving on the shore in a canoe and being greeted by Native Americans.

Visit the Mint website to see what is currently being minted in their commemorative coin program. You can also view both old and new commemorative coins in coin dealers' stores. You can also do your own research into what is significant about your state from material you can find in the public library or on the web. The topics are almost limitless.

Abraham Lincoln is an ideal subject for the 1918 Illinois commemorative half dollar, but a bust in this form would not be acceptable for the Statehood quarter. The 1921 Missouri Centennial half dollar makes a better statement, showing a frontiersman visiting with a Native American.

Selecting something appropriate and presenting it in a pleasing manner will be the real challenge for most would-be designers.

However you approach designing a coin for your state, or even if you only speculate on what could, or might, be done, you will enjoy learning more about your state, its history, and the many attractions it has to offer its citizens and tourists. You will also get much the same satisfaction from seeing, handling, and studying the Statehood quarters of all of the other 50 states. Save them, learn from them, trade them with your friends, and discuss them with your children. The 50 State Quarters program has much to offer everyone. Best of all there is the possibility of your design being selected as one to be used on a coin that will be seen and appreciated by millions of Americans.

Mistakes to be avoided are typified by the 1936 Wisconsin commemorative half dollar that showed a beaver, in punning reference to the miners of that state. The 1860 gold ten-dollar coin of Colorado was designed by someone who had never seen Pikes Peak and thought it should look like a pyramid.

Your design suggestions should be submitted to the state governor's office in a uniform manner for the evaluation process. You can draw your own outline or use the standard form recommended by the Mint. The design must not exceed the area reserved for the image in the center of the coin. Outer areas are for use by the Mint in adding standard wording.

The following template may be reproduced, copied, or enlarged as necessary for use as a workspace in preparing a design for submission to the governor. All regulations must be followed carefully to insure that any submission is given consideration.

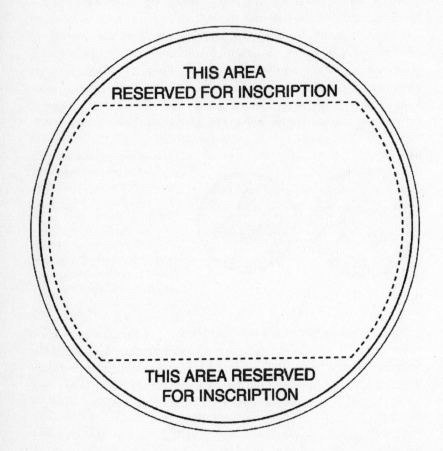

5

Collecting Coins as a Hobby

Collectible hobbies are among the most prevalent of all forms of recreation. Meeting a challenge and doing something that only a few others have been able to accomplish is one of the main goals of a collectible hobby. Owning a rare coin that is one of only a half dozen in the world gives a sense of pride that brings attention to the lucky holder. For others, the knowledge that buying a rare collectible has been a good investment is doubly rewarding.

The single-minded person who does not extend an outside interest to the world around is destined to miss out on some of the most enjoyable moments in life. It matters less what one chooses for a hobby than that it is something enjoyable and rewarding to the individual. For some the thrill of restoring a classic auto to its original form is exhilarating. For others, finding a rare old coin that completes a collection is just as exciting. Some people get the same thrill out of finding a special seashell. In every case, it seems to be the achievement, rather than the value, time, or money, that is the rewarding part of each success.

The recreational value of any hobby is another reason that cannot be overlooked. It draws countless people into the arena, and proves time and time again that getting away from a daily routine and into a world the collector can control is therapeutic. There is something about the lifestyle of a collector that is different from others. They are more active, more outgoing, healthier, and frankly more interesting than our other friends.

But can a hobby actually add years to your life? Most authorities agree that any absorbing hobby can help, and certainly will not harm one in any way. A study of coin collectors in their eighties and nineties shows that many people do indeed seem to remain more active than others who have not carried on an interest in some such pastime.

Can coin collecting help you to live longer? Those who have tried it say so, and there are many who can back up that claim. Apparently the gods still do not subtract from man's allotted days those hours spent in any peaceful recreation.

COINS AS MONEY; COINS AS COLLECTIBLES

Coins—as artifacts that trace the history and artistry of the world since ancient times—fascinate numismatists, or coin collectors. Some coins are known to have been made over 2,600 years ago. The possibilities of tying coins to history over this vast expanse of time are unlimited, and make the world of coins a treasure house of information about art, history, and technology. A stamp or a painting might show and commemorate some historical event, but a coin could have been present at the actual happening.

Very old coins are artifacts that should be preserved in museums like other ancient objects. Most historical museums do use coins to augment other displays, and when seen in that context they are very much treasured for their educational value. But coins are unlike other museum objects in that they were made in great numbers, and many of them have been preserved over the centuries. The happy result of this is that many of those same artifacts can actually be owned by private collectors where they can be appreciated and shared by a wide audience.

For many people an interest in collecting modern coins can be just as rewarding as searching for ancient artifacts. The procedure is the same. Coins are accumulated, organized, and protected in an orderly manner. In doing this, a mirror of history, both current and past, is being preserved for others to learn from in the future. There is a great satisfaction in knowing that one's efforts to save a bit of the past in an organized manner might be appreciated by generations to come.

Throughout much of recorded history, coins have taken part in actual events or have been used as a means of spreading news of those happenings. In times before there were newspapers or means of mass communications, coins were often used as a way of conveying news to people in remote regions. The image of a new emperor, the current favorite god or goddess, and news of a war or victory were prevalent themes on coins for hundreds of years. The panorama of events chronicled on coins that have been used since 650 B.C. offers a very real connection with those events that can take one on a journey back in time.

Have you ever wondered what Queen Cleopatra of Egypt really looked like? Was she the raving beauty we see in movies or read about in novels? Did she actually exist? Those questions can all be answered by looking at one of the many coins she had made for use in her kingdom. Yes, many of those coins still exist today and can be found in museums and private collections.

Coins were there when the Bible was written. There are many passages in the Bible that mention coins or the use of money, because that is a very essential part of daily life. Wages for "the laborers in the vineyard," the parable of the "lost coin," and the "coin of tribute" shown to Jesus are but a few of the many passages that refer to actual coins that can be identified and collected through diligent searching.

Undoubtedly the most famous coins of all in the Bible are the "thirty pieces of silver" that were paid for the betrayal of Jesus. Do they actually exist? Well, perhaps not the same thirty pieces, but coins just like them do. Coins that were used during the lifetime of Jesus may very well have been spent by any one or more prominent Biblical figures. Such coins not only still exist, but they are not so rare or expensive that they are all in museums. A nice specimen of a silver *tetradrachm* of Tyre can be purchased for about $600. The coin is not only a historical treasure, it is also a large and attractive piece that shows the head of Melcarth on one side and an eagle on the other.

Ferdinand and Isabella of Spain financed Columbus's voyage of discovery to the New World with some of these large gold coins that show their portraits as benevolent monarchs.

The journey through history that coins can provide does not stop with a chronicle of wars, kings, and kingdoms. It also provides an unmatchable link to the artistry of each period of style and mode. Want to see how Queen Elizabeth I looked and dressed? Her coins tell the whole story. Were the Greeks really better artisans than the Romans? It is easy to see the differences in the style and modeling of their coins. Did artists of the Renaissance influence coins of that period? How have modern artists changed the faces of coins today? Answers to all of these questions can be verified by viewing the thousands of such coins that have survived for us to enjoy as collectors.

POPULARITY AND GROWTH OF COIN COLLECTING

There are hundreds of reasons why people collect coins. Everyone seems to have a slightly different approach to enjoying the hobby, but there are four reasons that seem to be universal: pride of ownership, a thirst for knowledge, a desire to preserve the past, and the profit motive. Each of those motivators can be a powerful incentive, but few people collect solely for one reason. The most common theme to coin collecting seems to be a desire to form a complete set of one or more kinds of coins. The urge to achieve completeness and own every possible date, mintmark, or minor variety of some type of coin is probably the most compelling factor for most collectors.

No one knows exactly when coin collecting became a popular hobby. It is certain that there were collectors of old and unusual coins over 2,000 years ago. Why the ancient Greeks collected coins is uncertain, but it is easy to speculate that they appreciated the superb artistry of those coins then, just as we do now. It is also evident that some of the older designs were copied and reused by later coin engravers who must have been inspired by seeing the old pieces.

The silver tetradrachm of Athens was used as a standard for trade throughout the ancient world for over 200 years. This piece showing the goddess Athena and her owl, both symbols of wisdom, was minted around 440 B.C.

By the Middle Ages, coins were being used universally, and were appreciated for their artistry and as artifacts of past civilizations. They were often collected by the aristocracy in an effort to preserve things that were unusual or of great value. In time some of those collections became national treasures or part of the national museums of various European countries.

Later, in the seventeenth and eighteenth centuries, it was considered fashionable for wealthy European families to have a curio cabinet that included a selection of old coins. Some of the more aggressive collectors formed extensive collections that thankfully preserved many coins that might have been otherwise lost through attrition or melting.

Oddly enough, it was the shortage of copper coins in England in the late 1700s that started the wave of interest in coin collecting that has lasted up to the present. The price of copper had kept the British government from making enough coins to accommodate the needs of daily commerce, and to make matters worse, counterfeiters took this opportunity to issue thousands of lightweight imitation coins. Merchants who were desperate for some means of making change were forced to use the false coins for lack of anything better.

The situation in England changed somewhat in 1792, when a few merchants began making their own coins to give out to customers as change. The homemade coins served a dual purpose. They were a handy means of making change, and they also contained an advertising message for the company that issued them. What's more, the tokens eventually had to be returned to the same store to be redeemed. In time thousands of businesses issued their private tokens, most of which had unique designs that were attractive and interesting.

A virtual flood of privately made merchants' tokens was put into circulation during the period 1792 to 1794. It was then that collectors began saving as many different designs as they could find, and a wave of interest in coin collecting began throughout England. To add to the excitement, some of the manufacturers of the merchants' tokens began making special fancy pieces just for collectors. Some of those were made up using an obverse die of one token, combined with the reverse of a different token.

Serious coin collecting did not become fashionable in the United States until somewhere around 1830. There were a few collectors as long ago as presidents Thomas Jefferson and John Quincy Adams, both of whom saved coins as part of their other accumulations of interesting *objets d'art*, but there were only a few wealthy collectors who seriously tried to put together sets of United States coins.

The Civil War, and all of the numismatic innovations that it brought, was the great turning point in collecting interest in America. It was in that period that Federal paper money was issued for the first time, and along with that there was an extensive production of small denomination script called "fractional currency." The value of those notes ranged from three cents to fifty cents, and they were made in a variety of designs. Those unusual notes, together with the seemingly endless array of Confederate States paper money, were fertile fields for collecting opportunities.

The Civil War also brought about new coins and new coin designs. In 1864 a two-cent coin made its appearance, bearing the religious motto IN GOD WE TRUST, which slowly came into use and eventually spread to all other U.S. coins. In 1865 a three-cent coin made of nickel was introduced, and later the small-size cent, which had been in use since 1857, was also redesigned and made thinner.

With so many numismatic items to choose from, the hobby grew in popularity over the next quarter century and a number of books on the subject were written to stimulate interest and answer the many questions of concern to collectors. At that time there were no records of how many coins had been made in each year, or even what kinds of coins were issued. There was speculation about some dates of certain denominations that could not easily be found, but no one really knew what had or had not been made at any of the United States Mints.

The demand for information about coins as a collectible hobby was met by a few of the established collectors who had learned through experience, and who were skilled in writing books and articles on the subject. Others saw a business opportunity in buying and selling old coins, and established themselves as dealers and auctioneers. Much of the information about coins that was available to collectors of that time came from editorial comments in auction catalogs, a few books on the subject, and from sales catalogs and bulletins devoted to the hobby. Much of the available information was a mixture of half-truths and speculation.

The American Numismatic Society was founded in 1857 and began preserving coins, information, and reference materials in all areas of numismatics. It published articles and books that were available to its members. It was, and still is, an organization of researchers and students whose objectives are to study, locate, and preserve historical numismatic data. The very similar American Numismatic Association, which was founded in 1891, took on a slightly different role and became a national organization for coin collectors and hobbyists. In time a flood of high-quality literature from both the A.N.A. and the A.N.S. caught up with the demand for information, and by 1920 the lure of numismatics was in full swing throughout the country and throughout the world.

COLLECTING COMES OF AGE IN AMERICA

During the Great Depression, from 1929 to 1934, few Americans could afford to collect coins, but those who had collections found them to be a source of wealth that was easily converted into the necessities of life. Several large collections were sold at that time, and some others were formed by accumulating coins that were being sold at bargain prices. Throughout all of those hard times interest in coins remained high, and people turned to collectible hobbies as a rewarding and enjoyable form of recreation.

When the nation began its recovery from the Depression in the early 1930s, an even more intense interest in coin collecting developed. Much of that new activity was due to products that were introduced to the market by Whitman Publishing Company, a mass-market producer of children's books and games. One of the items they designed was a board punched with holes that would hold one each of all of the Lincoln cents or one each of the older Indian Head cents. The boards were of a size that would fit in a standard picture frame. The "game" was to find all of the coins, put them in the holder, and hang the frame as a wall decoration.

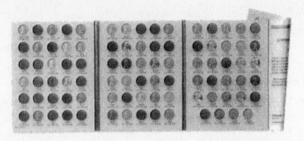

The hobby of coin collecting was advanced by the introduction of the Whitman® coin folder in 1938. It soon took the place of the old coin board that was large and bulky.

In time the coin boards came to be seen as a necessary aid to coin collecting, and they were redesigned to a more convenient size and form that could be folded in thirds for easy storage and to better protect the coins. As interest grew, more coin series and denominations were added to the Whitman selection of "coin folders," and several books were created to answer collectors' questions about the various coins that they were saving.

Two coin books that were introduced in the mid-1940s have continued to be updated and published each year and still serve as standard references for information about United States coins. Both of these books, The *Handbook of United States Coins* and *A Guide Book of United States Coins*, were originally authored by R. S. (Richard) Yeoman, and have been edited by Kenneth Bressett since 1974. The *Handbook*, usually called the "Blue Book" because of the color of its cover, is a basic reference to all American coins made since 1616. This book lists every item by date and mintmark, and shows each coin's approximate wholesale value in up to seven grades of condition.

The prices shown in the Blue Book are averages of what dealers will actually pay for coins that they want to purchase. It is different from most other coin books that usually list the retail price of coins, or what dealers charge for the coins they sell.

The *Guide Book*, known as the "Red Book," is a similar book for collectors that deals with the retail value of all American coins. It is much more detailed than the *Handbook* and contains useful information on all areas of United States coins. Special sections in both the Red Book and

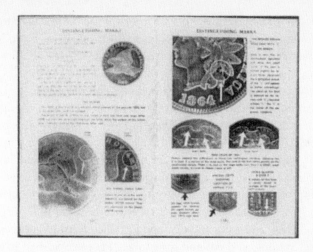

the Blue Book describe the coins that were used by colonial settlers and those that were made and used during the gold rush in California. Each of these books answers the questions most often asked by beginners, and contains information that is useful even for seasoned dealers.

When the economy began to settle down after World War II, and people got back to a more normal way of life, an even more intense interest in coin collecting arose throughout the country. People tired of war were looking for forms of recreation that would take their minds off the past decade. They began collecting by searching through coins found in circulation and looking for whatever was unusual. At that time it was possible to find just about every date and mint of all U.S. coins going back as far as the Barber issues of the late nineteenth century. It was great fun, but the fun was just beginning.

Starting around 1960, the real boom in coin collecting got underway. Coin books and coin collecting folders and albums were widely distributed through bookstores, novelty shops, coin dealers, clubs, and individuals. The end of finding scarce dates in circulation was in sight, and the hunt was on to see that no valuable coin went unnoticed. Prices being paid for those coins were beginning to escalate, and people everywhere were starting to think of old coins as something of value to be treasured and saved.

Over the following two decades interest in coins changed for many people from a simple hobby to a form of speculation or investment. It was becoming evident that many coins had a tendency to go up in value faster than other investments and that almost every scarce or rare coin could later be sold for more money than it cost just a few years earlier. The big winners in this bonanza were those collectors who had put together careful collections in the period from 1965 to 1975 and had saved them as prized possessions without any thought of a profit.

By 1980, when coin dealers and collectors began popping up everywhere, it was almost too late to get in on that phase of the hobby. It was during this time that the Hunt brothers made their famous move on the futures market in an attempt to drive up the price of silver. The beginning of the decade was also a time of hyperinflation, burgeoning prices for silver and gold, and demand for all collectibles like coins, old porcelain, stamps, and colored gemstones. People who had made fortunes on the rising market suddenly found that this was not a game that could go on forever. The value of all collectibles is based on supply and demand. When the demand began to waver, prices began to drop just as fast. By 1983 the rush to invest in rare coins cooled, and people once again began to appreciate them for their beauty and historical value.

In the intervening years from the mid-1980s to the end of the century, participation in coin collecting matured in many ways. It became much more clearly divided into segments of interest that appealed to various types of coin buyers. At one end of the spectrum is a limited number of museums and research students who are principally concerned with the study and preservation of historical treasures. At the other end there are thousands of everyday people who acquire coins in one way or another for the sheer fun of it without regard for value or anything else other than pride of ownership. In between is a vast array of collectors with every level of interest from serious investing, to searching for the latest issues of Statehood quarters.

From ancient times, when coins were first saved as records of significant and pleasing designs, to the present, where coins are most frequently saved as a recreational hobby, one thing has remained constant: the beauty and lore of those old, rare, and unusual coins hold a fascination for everyone.

Coin collecting is as rewarding and entertaining a hobby today as it has been for the past several hundred years. It is not a simple, passive diversion, but one that kindles the imagination and interest in things historical and beautiful. A well-formed collection of coins and other numismatic items can provide a lifetime of enjoyment and a legacy for future generations. The hobby should not be entered into lightly, but with the fire and conviction of a dedicated curator of a great treasure.

Beginning collectors will profit from investigating the background and history of the coins they accumulate. These are not just inanimate objects akin to other worldly goods. They are a mirror of history and art that tell the story of mankind over the past 2,600 years, reflecting the economic struggles, wars, prosperity, and creativity of every major nation on earth. We are but the custodians of these historical relics, and must appreciate and care for them while they are in our possession. Those who treat rare coins with the consideration and respect they deserve will profit in many ways, not the least of which can be in the form of a sound financial return on the investment of time and money.

YOU CAN FIND COINS EVERYWHERE

Just about everybody has a few odd coins stashed away somewhere. They may not be collectors, but for one reason or another most people tend to save any coin that does not seem to be ordinary or spendable. Perhaps it is a foreign coin that somehow got passed in change, or a bus token or an old penny that looks different because of the wheat ears on the reverse. Whatever the reason for saving those odd pieces, a person usually never just throws them away. They are money, and it takes a lot of courage to destroy any kind of money.

Collectors usually begin their hobby by looking at all of the different kinds of coins they can locate, regardless of what they are or where they may be found. That doesn't mean that you will be able to acquire all of those coins, but looking at everything available does give you a broad sense of what may be around, and how difficult or easy it is to find such things. You will quickly notice that coins found in pocket change are mostly of recent vintage and probably of little value to building a collection.

Is it worth the effort to check your daily stash of pocket change?

Should you inspect every coin that you receive in change at the grocery store? Hasn't someone else already gone over every coin in circulation and pulled out all the good dates? While there are no absolute answers to these questions, it's always a good rule to look at every coin that passes through your hands. There is no telling when or where something unusual will come along, and while there are many other collectors also looking, you can be the lucky one who is first to spot something of exceptional value.

There was a time when collectors could find just about every date and mintmark of every kind of coin in circulation. Even old Barber design coins dating back to the eighteenth century were still in circulation in the 1940s and '50s, and it was not unusual to occasionally find scarce dates that were worth a considerable premium. Yes, that was a great way to build a collection, and it was something that appealed to both young and old alike. Searching for all those different dates was a challenging and rewarding hobby, but alas those days are gone.

One of the things that changed over the years was the trend to keep the same design on United States coins for long periods of time. Coins tend to stay in circulation as long as the design does not change. Take, for instance, the Barber coins that were made from 1892 to 1916. They continued to circulate for 40 years or more because they were familiar and seemingly of no particular worth beyond their face value. They began to be appreciated only when they were replaced by coins of other designs, or lost through wear and attrition.

Things are not much different today. It seems natural to see coins in change that are 40 or even 50 years old. They do not look unusual to us because they are of the same design as the others that we use on a daily basis. If one does not stop and inspect the date, those old coins go unnoticed. But spot an old coin of an obsolete design, like a Buffalo nickel, in change, and everyone will stop and take a closer look at it. This tendency to ignore what seems commonplace has led to a generation that does not spend time looking for unusual coins in change, and with that goes lost opportunity.

A good example of the value of carefully inspecting the coins in your pocket is the experience of a Maine collector who always checked his change for scarce dates. Most of what he found had little premium value, but one day in 1998 he was rewarded with a 1972 cent that just didn't look right. When he got it home, he studied it carefully and found that it had a fully doubled date, and was in fact a variety worth over $100.

It would not be fair to describe the "good old days" of coin collecting without commenting on the fact that while it was possible to find occasional valuable coins in change, most of what was available was worth only face value at the time. The fun in finding those coins was in being able to form sets of all the different dates and kinds of pieces that were in circulation. Most of them became valuable only after they were long out of use and no longer easily available. It seems likely that there may never again be a time quite like the opportunistic days before World War II, but it is also good to consider that there could be similar opportunities today that are going unappreciated.

Most countries used silver in part of their national coinage until as recently as 1964. It was not until the price of silver began to rise beyond the face value of those coins that substitutes had to be made. Nearly all coins are now merely tokens with no intrinsic value, and thus they have no chance of increasing in worth because of any higher cost of the materials from which they are made. That's the unfortunate side of current coins. The good news is that there are many of the old silver coins still sitting around in drawers and boxes, waiting to be rediscovered by some active collector who can appreciate the value of those old treasures. The coins may be forgotten, but they are not gone from existence. There are plenty of them still in hiding.

Chances are that you have never found a silver coin in your pocket change. When they went out of use in 1965, many of them were immediately pulled from circulation by sharp-eyed collectors and anyone well informed about the spiraling cost of silver. Within ten years nearly all were gone from active use as money, and most were shipped off to the smelters for melting. Those who were lucky enough to get in on the action found that they could often buy silver coins at face value and sell them for a profit ranging from 3 percent in the early days to ten times face value at one point.

It is no wonder that most of those old silver coins are now gone from active use, but that does not mean that they are not available. Many people never got around to having their accumulation of silver coins melted. Others waited in hopes of even higher profits, and some people wanted to preserve specimens for the future. Whatever the reasons, there are still many large and small hoards of silver coins hidden away in drawers, boxes, and attics. Some are long forgotten, some are just waiting to be appreciated by a new generation of collectors.

What kinds of coins are in those hoards? The answer to this may amaze you. When silver went out of circulation in the late 1960s it was almost as if time was frozen at that point, and whatever had been in use was set aside without regard to dates, mintmarks, types, or rarity. Many of the old Barber design silver coins were still in circulation at the time, and it was normal to see Mercury dimes, Liberty Standing quarters, or Liberty Walking half dollars in daily change. The Franklin half dollar was, of course, in use everywhere and not uncommon to find in nearly new condition. All of those coins were suddenly taken from circulation and preserved in whatever groups were not sent to the melting pots.

At one point the value of silver reached $50 per ounce, and at that time it became profitable to melt many old coins that had some significant numismatic value. The pity is that many such coins were melted, but a few did manage to escape the fiery death and were set aside in hopes that they would be worth even more in the future. Old designs, scarce dates, commemorative coins, and choice condition United States and foreign silver coins were all suddenly gone from sight, but almost magically preserved in time capsules that today lie hidden and sometimes almost forgotten in the most unlikely places.

Rather than lament the "good old days," when great coins could be found in circulation, it would serve a beginning collector well to go out looking for some of the old hoards of silver, copper, and even gold coins that are now becoming available from a new generation of owners. Searching through some of those accumulations, which are often held by family members and friends, may be a golden opportunity for anyone wanting to fill in a collection or to find rare and valuable dates. Such untapped sources may also yield any number of unusual varieties that were not even known to collectors 25 years ago.

DON'T FORGET TO CHECK YOUR CHANGE

It is also true that there are some interesting and scarce coins that are still in circulation and waiting to be found by anyone with enough curiosity to look for them. Every beginning collector starts by checking for unusual coins in their daily change. Make it a habit to scan every handful of coins passed to you. You will soon learn to spot anything that does not look "normal," and you can set those coins aside to be studied more carefully later. Anything that is shiny and new should be saved in a special place so that nothing will happen to it before it can be compared to any other similar coins in your collection.

Can you tell why this 1969-S Lincoln cent is now worth over $1,000? It will pay to look for one in your change.

You should save at least one specimen of every coin in the highest quality that you can find. If you do not want to accumulate duplicates of common dates, be sure that the one you save is always the nicest. Do not settle for nicks or marks on any of the common pieces of recent years. You will almost always find nicer pieces later with enough searching, but in the beginning it will not hurt to save anything that looks different until you can properly classify everything and be sure that you have not missed some important feature.

Some people collect only a few different types of coins like cents or nickels, while others attempt to save one of each denomination, date and type. There are no rules or norms, so everyone feels free to do whatever seems best for them. Most people like to start with one series and then build up from there according to available time, money, and interest. All things being equal, a good beginning series would be the

Washington quarter series. It is one that can bring hours of pleasure in pursuing, and the reward of being able to fully complete the collection from circulation or through a few purchases. A completed collection can be worth anywhere from a couple hundred dollars to several thousand dollars depending on the limits one sets as to the condition of each coin.

Washington quarters were made nearly every year from 1932 to the present. That makes it a long and continuous series with lots of dates and mintmarks to look for. The coins are large and are made of either silver (1932–1964) or copper-nickel (1965 to date), so they are attractive and easy to see and handle. They wear well in circulation, so it is easy to find nice examples of nearly all of the recent dates, and if you are lucky enough to acquire a hoard of old silver coins, you should be able to locate nearly all of the older dates and mintmarks. You may also be able to spot some of the unusual designs that have letters or dates that are slightly doubled and are of such high interest and value to collectors today.

In a sense, collecting Washington quarters provides all of the basic ingredients of training, skills, and knowledge that one needs to successfully go on to any other area of United States numismatics. The same could be true of Lincoln cents or Jefferson nickels, but the Washington quarter series has so many dates, mintmarks, and minor varieties that it offer some things to look for that are lacking in other series. Thus they are highly recommended as an ideal starting point. They are also a series that is destined to receive much attention well into the future, because they were forerunners to the series of Statehood quarters that have captured the attention of nearly everyone since their appearance in 1999.

6

Caring for Your Collection

Building a valuable coin collection is fun, but it can also become a nightmare when something damaging happens to your coins. As sturdy as coins may seem, they are actually very fragile and can be easily damaged by improper handling or storage.

One of the most common errors in taking care of coins is the myth that well cleaned, shiny coins are more desirable than those that are old and tarnished. Yes, those coins seem much more attractive, but when coins are improperly cleaned they can be easily scratched and damaged. A harshly cleaned coin is always worth less than one that is natural and untouched. The best advice is *never attempt to clean any valuable coin*. You can always have a coin cleaned professionally later if it absolutely needs it, but you can never undo the harm that inexperienced cleaning may do to your coins.

You should also take precautions to see that your coins are carefully handled by anyone who inspects them. Friends who do not know the value of old coins can be careless when viewing your treasures, so don't hesitate to tell them how important it is to keep them free from marks and abrasions. Dropping a coin on a hard surface is just about the worst thing that you can do to it.

It is just as important to make sure that your valuable coins are stored in a secure place. A bank storage box is ideal. If that is not an option, be sure that they are kept in an inconspicuous place where they will be missed by any intruder. Also be sure that coins are stored in a place that is at a constant room temperature and free from excessive humidity. Your attic and basement, which are the two most frequent hiding places, are without doubt the worst possible choices.

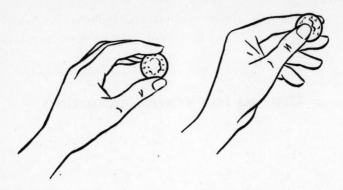

Don't take chances. There is only one correct way to hold a coin. It's the mark of a competent and wise collector.

The absolute rule that everyone must follow is to always hold every coin by the edge, and never touch the face, or flat surface, of the piece. This is essential. There is no excuse for anyone ever holding a coin in a way that could impress a fingerprint on the surface. To be even safer, you can, and should, use white gloves while handling valuable Uncirculated coins. Some people substitute thin Latex gloves and think them safer because they are not as slippery as linen. Others find them awkward and harder to use. Both offer a degree of safety that is better than taking a chance of "fingering" a valuable coin.

A fingerprint on a coin's surface might not seem like such a terrible thing, but it can be severely damaging to an otherwise uncirculated piece. The oils, acids, and salts that are present on a person's skin easily attack the delicate luster of a new coin. Simply touching an uncirculated coin will leave traces of those contaminates on the surface that will eat into the finish. The "fingerprint" will not be seen at first, but in about two weeks it will begin to blossom and become clear in every minor detail. The tragedy of these unsightly marks is that they will never go away except when worn off by circulation or harsh abrasive cleaning.

Almost as important as proper handling is making sure that you always work over a padded surface. A jeweler's tray is ideal, but not always convenient or available. Next best is a cloth pad or folded towel. Remind yourself that no one is exempt from occasionally dropping a coin. It happens to the best numismatists and seems inevitable. Dropping a coin on a padded surface will do little or no harm, and may save lots of aggravation. For added protection, always view coins over a carpeted floor.

If the coin you are inspecting is in a plastic holder it is usually best not to remove it. There may be reasons to take a coin out of its holder, but often this is inviting danger. Never touch or rub the surface of a coin with your hands or anything abrasive. Even some paper and plastic holders can mar an uncirculated coin if not used properly.

For some reason there is a natural tendency to rub the surface of a coin with the thumb to make it clearer and shinier. This is one of the worst things you could ever do. The trick is to treat all coins as if they are extremely fragile. They are.

Have you ever seen an uncirculated coin with tiny black spots on the surface? Those are moisture spots, and they are caused by someone coughing or breathing on the coin. Wear a surgical mask if you have a cold and just can't wait to look at your coins. Those spots can also be caused by moisture condensation if coins are moved from a cold place to a warm room.

Be especially vigilant when handling other people's coins. I have seen rim nicks that have lessened the value of coins by thousands of dollars . . . all due to careless handling or dropping a coin on a hard surface. It only takes a few extra minutes to be safe rather than sorry.

ALBUMS AND HOLDERS

The importance of building your collection with coins in the finest possible condition cannot be overemphasized, but preserving them is equally important. Coins should not be abused, mishandled, or stored loosely with other coins that can cause nicks, dents, or scratches. Careful storage in specially made holders, albums, or folders is essential to preserving high-quality coins. When handling coins you should always hold then between two fingers on the rim, and only remove them from holders and albums when necessary.

No matter how well preserved, coins are susceptible to oxidation and tarnish. If you live in a community near salt water, where the air is polluted by factories, or with excessive humidity, you must constantly protect your coins from these harmful elements. The only sure way to preserve a coin's natural condition is to seal it in an airtight container. This, however, is generally impractical, as is embedding a coin in plastic or sealing it in aluminum or tin foil. The chief drawback to this kind of protection is that you are not able to get to the coin when you wish to examine or display it.

Modern technology has produced a variety of plastics that are suitable for protecting coins. The popular 2" x 2" coin holder made of polystyrene plastic with an airtight seal is the most practical container for a single coin. The Whitman® Snap Lock plastic holder made of inert polystyrene is one of the best. These holders are suitable for display purposes, are a convenient size for storage, and are easily opened for coin removal. The special construction of these holders offers nearly complete protection for an indefinite period of storage.

Less valuable coins can be stored in 2" x 2" cardboard coin mounts, or paper coin envelopes. All of these items may be purchased through any coin dealer or hobby supply store. One of the major advantages of using 2" x 2" paper envelopes is that any information about the coin may be written on the outside of each envelope. It is also possible, and fun, to use computer-generated printed labels to identify coins in any of these holders. There are computer programs designed to catalog and inventory your collection and print labels whenever needed.

A variety of containers are available for storing individual envelopes or plastic holders. Many of the trays and storage boxes used for storing photographic slides can be adapted for storing coins. Coin dealers generally offer specially constructed cardboard or plastic storage boxes made specifically for coin use. Be careful to select one that is as nearly airtight as possible. If you plan to store your coins for a long period of time in one of these containers, it should be sealed with tape to add further protection. You should also examine your coins periodically to see that no harmful tarnish has developed; but of course, you will want to look at your coins from time to time anyway.

There are many types of holders and albums that will hold complete sets or series of coins. Plastic pages, similar to plastic 2" x 2" individual coin holders, are available for complete sets of each denomination. They are by far the most attractive and protective, but also cost the most. Polystyrene coin holders for Proof Sets or Mint Sets are also available, and offer a convenient method of storing all the coins of a single year.

Coin *folders* and *albums* are the most commonly used storage holders for coin sets. The Whitman Classic Album consists of individual pages with openings for one date or mint of each coin in the series. They are made to hold sets of all of the modern coins. Specialty holders are also available for type sets and older coins. The openings in these albums are covered on both sides with removable plastic slides. This arrangement provides not only great protection to the coins, but also a convenient way to display them; both sides of all coins are visible. It is also easy to remove individual pages for exhibition and display. A simple screw post holds pages in place so that they can be removed, replaced, or added to the basic album.

A less expensive but still practical means of storing sets of United States coins is the Whitman blue coin folder. Most collectors begin the hobby by purchasing folders for a set of current Lincoln cents, Jefferson nickels, or higher denominations if their funds permit. One coin of each date and mint can be inserted into the openings of these folders. A brief history of each coin series and an indication of the number of coins issued each year are included in this convenient method of organizing and storing a collection.

• • •

Each year an alarming number of Mint State and Proof coins are ir-
reparably damaged through improper storage. In addition to causing huge
losses in value, this phenomenon has a significant impact on the availability of desirable high-grade coins. Often it is you, the unsuspecting collector, who suffers when assuming that a coin will be immune from harm as
long as it is stored in a popular type of coin holder, such as an album, roll
tube, or single coin container, then placed in a safe or vault. This is a very
dangerous and naive misconception. The fact is, anyone who does not
seek to understand the proper methods of coin preservation runs a high
risk of serious damage and loss of value. Such damage can actually begin
in a matter of months from the time a coin is improperly stored.

Metals are found in their natural ore state in combination with other
elements, which include oxides, the chemical compounds formed by the
reaction of metal with oxygen in the air. Before the coining process can
begin, the metal is refined and purified, thus removing the oxides. This
pure metal is chemically unstable and tends to revert to its former natural ore state by recombining with oxygen and reforming the oxides.
Newly minted coins immediately start to acquire an oxide layer, which
begins at a thickness of millionths of a millimeter and is invisible to the
naked eye. In the early stages, oxides on coins aid in protection against
other forms of corrosion and do not hide the luster of the coin surface.

As time passes, the oxide layers increase in thickness and are added
to by various types of contaminants, forming uneven coatings. Often
called tarnish, these layers become visible with time and can lead to the
formation of dark spots and other discoloration. Later, actual pitting of

the metal surface may take place. Naturally, such advanced forms of corrosion are not always removable and may substantially lower the numismatic value of a coin. It is important to protect coins from all forms of corrosion, and this may be accomplished by giving careful attention to proper storage in a humidity-controlled environment, and with the use of coin containers that can form a barrier between the coin and any outside elements.

Whether coins are stored in your home or in a safe deposit box, care must be taken to insure that the environment is suitable. Moisture and heat are enemies of coin metals because they promote oxidation and corrosion. If coins are kept at home, they should be stored in a room that is comfortable for you. Namely, one which is cool and not humid, and within the normal range of room temperatures.

The same precautions apply when a safe is used for home storage. Despite the perceived strength of a cement floor, never put a safe in a basement that is not protected against dampness or flooding. Never keep coins in an attic where the heat can build up to extremes in summer. If coins are stored in a bank, select a vault room where it is cool and dry, and preferably air-conditioned in the summer, because air conditioning also removes humidity from the air.

ADDITIONAL PROTECTION

Some of the problems with humidity can be reduced by storing coins in a place with relative humidity controls, but few of us have that luxury available either at home or in a bank vault. A compound known as "silica gel" offers a partial solution to this dilemma. Silica gel is a porous, granular, non-crystalline form of silica that is commonly used in many situations to help create a dry storage environment. It is cheap, easy to use, and can be fitted easily into nearly all kinds of cases and boxes in a home or in a bank vault.

It is not always easy to check on the effectiveness of silica gel stored with your coins to see if it is working. If coins are in a bank vault, you may forget to look in on them for months at a time. If you store paper money along with your coins, the silica could do more harm than good by drying out the paper. Be sure to read and follow all instructions that come with any product you choose.

INSURANCE AND RECORD-KEEPING

Insurance is as essential for protection of your valuable coins as are proper storage methods. This might not be important for a small accumulation of coins with minimal value, but if the value is significant to you, it's time to think about risk insurance. If you store your coins in a bank vault, you should purchase insurance that covers all risks such as theft, fire, water damage, and other perils, because the normal bank vault insurance coverage is only for dishonesty, negligence, and a few other risks.

Low-cost vault insurance is widely available from most major carriers. However, such insurance policies usually cover coins only when in the vault, and not outside or in transport to and from the bank. Coverage outside the vault is generally costly, often as much as 10 percent of the value insured per year.

If your coins are stored at home you can insure them through a special rider to your home policy. The cost of this will vary according to where and how the coins are stored and protected. Do not assume that your home policy will protect coins under the same terms as your other property. They are considered cash and may be appraised at face value. Check with your insurance agent to learn more about terms and conditions that may apply to coins and other collectibles that you store at home. Obviously, you must determine if the cost of such protection is warranted, but in all cases, some form of insurance is highly recommended. You should appraise your coins each year and update the insurance coverage for them as needed.

Keeping track of the value of your collection means that you will have to have a complete inventory of what you own. Making a list is easy, and it will not be an arduous task if you keep it up to date with each new purchase. You can use your computer to great advantage in making such lists, and a few special coin inventory programs (advertised in coin publications) are available for your convenience. It is extremely important to always have an inventory available in case of theft, damage, or even death. You will also need such records for tax purposes when it comes time to sell your collection or pass it on to someone else. You should be sure to include mention of your collection in your will to be sure that all of your wishes are followed at time of death. Taking care of this kind of paperwork is just as important as protecting a collection in all other ways.

When inventorying your collection you should keep a record of exactly what each item is, when and where you purchased it, the original cost, the current value, and where it is stored. A proper description of each piece would include the date, mintmark, metal, denomination, any special features, a catalog number if that is known, the condition or grade, and the country or issuing authority. If the piece is a token, medal, or some other numismatic item, that too should be noted. A typical entry might be something like this:

"United States. Five cents 1942-P. Silver wartime composition. Uncirculated. Purchased 1990 Ace Coin Co. for $5.00. Current (2000) Value $7.00"

STORING YOUR COINS

There are many surface contaminants that can find their way onto a coin and harm the metal if not removed. The most common are dirt, grease, oils, dust, and dandruff, all of which are often invisible to the naked eye. The minting process itself may leave deposits of grease from the dies or from other related machinery used to prepare the coins. Individuals may mishandle coins and deposit skin oils, or leave fingerprints on them. Also, some kinds of plastic holders can be a major source of contamination because of migrating chemical compounds from the plastic film.

If a coin has been improperly stored in the past or is corroded, it is important to remove any harmful surface contaminants before storing the coin. Coins purchased from a dealer will probably already have been treated if there were any problems. Common solvents such as alcohol and acetone may be safely used for this purpose, but even that kind of a bath is best left up to the more experienced professionals. Silver "dips" consisting of thiourea and dilute nitric acid are sometimes used by dealers to remove any surface pollution. However, the dips will also remove toning and oxide layers and expose the metal to atmospheric attack. Improperly used, dips can leave stains on coins.

Unless you have some special unique concerns about surface contaminants on the coins you intend to store, it is best to avoid handling them or attempting to clean them in any way before storage. Questions about problem coins are best left up to the judgment of experienced collectors or dealers. Consult with one of them before making any attempt to clean or improve your coins.

You may also be unaware that certain types of coin housing products specifically designed to protect coins can actually cause serious damage. In the past some coin holders were made of polyvinyl chloride (PVC), a type of soft plastic film that had a tendency to release harmful gases under heat and pressure. Coins stored in those vinyl holders often suffer from damage caused by contact with polyvinyl chloride. There are very few such holders on the market today, but collectors should avoid using any product that is known to contain polyvinyl plastic.

Unfortunately there is no single "perfect" way to store coins. Most collectors use a variety of different holders and protective containers to house their valuable items. I have seen them all, and I have come to understand that whatever pleases each individual may be what is best for them. Some like to show their coins to friends and need holders that protect the coins from handling but are easy to see. Others have their most valuable coins sealed in plastic "slabs," and store them in a bank vault. The single most important consideration is that coins should be shielded from moisture, air, and extremes of temperature. For maximum protection, I would recommend that coins be sealed in plastic holders, stored in an airtight plastic box that is kept in a bank vault. Even then they should be inspected two or three times each year to be sure that they have not deteriorated in any way.

Checklist of States and Mints

Date	State	P	D	Date	State	P	D
1999	Delaware	❏	❏	2004	Michigan	❏	❏
1999	Pennsylvania	❏	❏	2004	Florida	❏	❏
1999	New Jersey	❏	❏	2004	Texas	❏	❏
1999	Georgia	❏	❏	2004	Iowa	❏	❏
1999	Connecticut	❏	❏	2004	Wisconsin	❏	❏
2000	Massachusetts	❏	❏	2005	California	❏	❏
2000	Maryland	❏	❏	2005	Minnesota	❏	❏
2000	South Carolina	❏	❏	2005	Oregon	❏	❏
2000	New Hampshire	❏	❏	2005	Kansas	❏	❏
2000	Virginia	❏	❏	2005	West Virginia	❏	❏
2001	New York	❏	❏	2006	Nevada	❏	❏
2001	North Carolina	❏	❏	2006	Nebraska	❏	❏
2001	Rode Island	❏	❏	2006	Colorado	❏	❏
2001	Vermont	❏	❏	2006	North Dakota	❏	❏
2001	Kentucky	❏	❏	2006	South Dakota	❏	❏
2002	Tennessee	❏	❏	2007	Montana	❏	❏
2002	Ohio	❏	❏	2007	Washington	❏	❏
2002	Louisiana	❏	❏	2007	Idaho	❏	❏
2002	Indiana	❏	❏	2007	Wyoming	❏	❏
2002	Mississippi	❏	❏	2007	Utah	❏	❏
2003	Illinois	❏	❏	2008	Oklahoma	❏	❏
2003	Alabama	❏	❏	2008	New Mexico	❏	❏
2003	Maine	❏	❏	2008	Arizona	❏	❏
2003	Missouri	❏	❏	2008	Alaska	❏	❏
2003	Arkansas	❏	❏	2008	Hawaii	❏	❏

WHITMAN® COIN BOOKS & PRODUCTS

A Guide Book of United States Coins
The Official Red Book of U.S. Coins, 53rd Edition 2000
R. S. Yeoman
$12.95 hc, 0-307-48005-4, #48005-00
$8.95 coil bound, 0-307-48004-6, #48004-00

United States and Canada Coin Collector's Check List and Record Book
$3.25 pbk., 0-307-19099-4, #9091-8

Official A.N.A. Grading Standards for United States Coins, 5th Edition
$13.95 pbk., 0-307-09097-3, #9097-3

Coins: Questions & Answers
Clifford Mishler
$7.95 pbk., 0-307-09359-X, #9359

The Whitman Guide to Coin Collecting
Ken Bressett
$9.95 pbk., 0-307-48008-9, #48008-00

Photograde Coin Grading Guide, 18th Edition
James F. Ruddy
$10.95 pbk., 0-307-99361-2, #9361

Handbook of Ancient Greek and Roman Coins
Zander H. Klawans and K. E. Bressett (Editor)
$13.95 pbk., 0-307-09362-X, #9362

Guide Book of United States Currency, 3rd Edition
Kenneth Bressett
$15.95 pbk., 0-307-48003-8, #48003-00

Also available are coin folders, albums, starter sets, and a variety of storage boxes and holders.